CHRIST AND US

CHRIST
AND US

JEAN DANIÉLOU

A Translation of *Approches du Christ* by
WALTER ROBERTS

SHEED & WARD · NEW YORK

Nihil obstat: RICARDUS ROCHE, S.T.D., *Censor deputatus*
Imprimatur: ✠ FRANCISCUS, *Archiepiscopus Birmingamiensis*
datum Birmingamiae 3a Martii, 1961

232
D22aE

Second Printing, January 1962

Library of Congress Catalog Card Number 61-7294

Manufactured in the United States of America

IN MEMORIAM
MATRIS DILECTISSIMAE
QUAE DOCUIT MIHI
DILIGERE CHRISTUM

PREFACE

THE plan of this little book requires some brief justification. It would appear at first sight that it deals at the same time with heterogeneous subjects belonging to different disciplines. We pass successively from exegesis to dogmatic theology, from biblical theology to spirituality. There is a danger that this mixture of subjects will disconcert the reader. This is precisely the intention of the book. It aims at breaking down the compartments which, under the legitimate pretext of separating one method from another, eventually divide up the very subject with which they are concerned.

Let us clarify this statement. The historians strive to reconstruct the life of Jesus and to place it once more in its historical context, and do so by setting aside the supernatural element, as being foreign to their method. To this Jesus of history is opposed the Jesus of faith, the encounter with whom is a decisive event in personal life. Or again, in another perspective, it is recognized that there are in the life of Jesus certain outstanding divine interventions. And yet there is a refusal to recognize similar interventions in the sacraments of the Church or the inner life of souls. In the end, the diversity of these approaches only succeeds in partitioning Christ Himself, since each discipline only preserves that aspect of Him which corresponds to its intention.

Now it is precisely these divisions that are called in question in the present work. To paint a purely human portrait of Jesus, preserving only the acts of His humanity during His earthly life, is not only an abstraction, but treason. And conversely, to attach little importance to the Christ of history by concentrating exclusively on the existential experience of the encounter with Christ, is ultimately to call in question the historical objectivity of the Incarnation itself. Indeed it is easier to distinguish an empirical Jesus and a noumenal Jesus, and to concentrate on one or the other; but to do this is to remove the 'stumbling block' of the Incarnation.

In reality, the Jesus of history is already the Lord of faith, as the Lord of faith is still the Jesus of history. There is a strict continuity between the Word of God the Creator, the Wisdom that inspired the Prophets, the Child of Bethlehem, the Crucified Jesus of Golgotha, the Glorified Christ present in the Eucharist, the inward Master who teaches the saints. It is only a question, as Bérulle says, of different states of the incarnate Word. It is one and the same Word of God who is at the beginning, who will come again at the end, and who fills the whole space between.

Of this unfathomable richness of Christ, which passes all understanding, we wish at least to lose nothing that will help us to grasp certain truths. And it is here that a legitimate place may be found for a variety of approaches and methods. Everything is valuable that can lead us to a better understanding of Him the knowledge of whom is the one thing necessary. Thus we shall listen in turn to historians and theologians, exegetes and mystics. For it is the complementary quality of their views that will help us to glimpse the fullness of Christ.

This amounts to saying that the aim of the present work is to provide a kind of Summa. But it is also clear from what has been said that in each particular discipline it is only possible to indicate general tendencies. A reader who wishes to examine this or that question more thoroughly, or to find fuller justification for this or that statement, should consult more detailed works. It is to facilitate this research that bibliographies are given at the end of each chapter, offering suggestions for further reading. The book as a whole takes up again, on another subject, the plan of *God and Us*.

ACKNOWLEDGEMENT

ALL quotations from Holy Scripture in this work are taken from the version by the late Monsignor Ronald Knox, by kind permission of the Cardinal Archbishop of Westminster.

CONTENTS

CORRIGENDUM. On page 108, line 19, for 'peripheral' read 'outmoded'.

CHRIST AND US

CHAPTER I

THE HISTORICAL APPROACH

THE fact of Christianity provides in itself an irreducible
datum which everyone must one day encounter, and concerning which he must examine himself. But this fact can
be approached in various ways. It can be considered by
beginning with the present reality of the Church, inasmuch
as it represents in the world a power belonging to an order
which stands altogether apart, which demands to be understood and explained. It can be considered from the point
of view of personal existence, as an inward event, that of
the discovery of Christ giving life an entirely fresh significance. Finally it can be considered from the point of view
of the person of Jesus in His earthly life, as a historical
fact which we know through the medium of the documents
of the New Testament.

Each of these approaches is possible. And in this sense
the order of the chapters in this book could perfectly
well be changed round. It is a case like that of those
writings of Philo of Alexandria whose composition Père
Delcuve has shown to be circular, since what is described
as their beginning and end is only the point where the
circle has been cut so as to enable the matter to be set
out in due order. In particular, our final chapter on the
personal encounter with Christ might well have come first.
In some ways it would be more like the literary pattern of
the Gospels to speak first of the Divinity of Jesus, who is
the proper object of their declarations.

However, we have chosen to follow a different order, by approaching Christ in accordance with the very order of His manifestation. In this order, the first thing that appears is the fact of His entry into history—the person and the life of Jesus. In this historical entry, Christ reveals Himself as belonging at the same time to common humanity and to a higher realm. The two aspects are inseparably united in the warf and woof of His life. However, they must be studied separately—recognizing as we must that this separation is only an intellectual convention. Nothing would be more contrary to what is laid down in the Gospels than to isolate a human figure of Jesus from the divine interventions which the Gospels associate with Him.

. . . . .

In the perspective which we have chosen to present first—that of the manifestation of Christ—it is on the level of documents that this must be encountered. For documents are the sole means of access to the historical realities. This does not mean that historical realities are not capable of a certainty as great as that of the realities of mathematics or physics. It would be a distortion of the reason to suppose that this is the case. Historical certainties are just as absolute in their own sphere as mathematical certainties. But they require, to be securely established, the rigorous use of methods appropriate to their subject matter. This method is the critical examination of those documents that bear witness to them and of the reliance that can be placed upon these. So it is of this criticism that we must speak, to arrive with certainty at the person of Jesus in His historical reality.

One question which arises at the outset is that of the writings of the New Testament, namely, the extent to which they are historical documents in the ordinary sense of the word, that is, the extent to which they are a witness to historical events. In fact it is clear that these writings are not primarily historical works in the modern sense of the word, but the witness of the faith of the first Christian community. Can we, nevertheless, grasp through them something of the life of Jesus? The problem varies according to which New Testament writings we consider. It is mainly concerned with the Gospels. But we shall have something to say first of all about the Epistles of St. Paul, which raise the question in its most acute form.

St. Paul maintains an almost complete silence with regard to the historical events of the life of Jesus. The radical solution consists in saying that he knew nothing of the tradition about Jesus. This is the standpoint of Wrede, in his *Paulus*. It is likewise that of Alfaric in his study *Paul and Jesus*: 'A rapid survey of the Pauline passages in which it was thought that living memories of a historical Jesus could be seen will show that they are all on an ideal plane, completely foreign to history.'[1] But this is most unlikely. Paul was a contemporary of Jesus. If he was present at the martyrdom of Stephen, if he studied at the feet of Gamaliel, he must have lived at Jerusalem at the time of the Passion. However, it would be astonishing if he had known Jesus personally, since he never mentions this.

What is certain is that he was in contact with men who had lived with Jesus. At the very time when he was persecuting the Christians, he was meeting them in the synagogues, was hearing them speak of Christ. After his conversion, he was in contact with Peter in the course of his visits to Jerusalem (*Gal.* 2 [9]). So it is absolutely certain that he was acquainted with the life of Jesus. 'It is almost

[1] *Congrès d'histoire du christianisme, Jubilé Alfred Loisy*, II, 1928, p. 79.

inconceivable,' writes Fridrichsen, 'that the Apostle could have failed to be aware of what was said about the Messiah in Jerusalem, Damascus and Antioch.'[1] And the few very definite allusions which he makes to the Last Supper and the Resurrection appearances show that when he wishes he is quite capable of showing that he knows Christ according to the flesh as well as anyone else.

Why, then, does he not speak of this? Some have thought that it is because he attached no importance to such details. Thus Schweitzer holds that for Paul there is no connection between the period prior to the death and resurrection of the Lord and the new era in which salvation is accomplished. The human life of Jesus belongs to the old order, henceforth abolished. So it is no longer of any interest, and the Apostle ignores it deliberately. Schweitzer bases his argument on the famous text: 'Therefore, henceforward we do not think of anybody in a merely human fashion; even if we used to think of Christ in a human fashion, we do so no longer.'[2] Leisegang reaches a similar conclusion by referring to the historical Jesus and the Kyrios what Paul says of the natural man and the spiritual man.

This point of view goes too far in exaggerating Paul's disparagement of Christ during His earthly life. But it lies in the direction of the truth. It is certain that St. Paul, 'while he was thoroughly acquainted with the earthly life of Christ, said very little about it.'[3] But he had his reasons for this. The explanation is that in his opinion the whole emphasis should be placed on the kingship of Christ as being the essential object of faith. It was completely pointless to insist on the human details of the life of Jesus;

[1] *Le problème du miracle dans le christianisme primitif*, p. 25.
[2] 2 Cor. 5 [16].   [3] Anton Fridrichsen, op. cit., p. 19.

first, because they were not questioned in Paul's circle, and second, because they were not what mattered most. What did matter was the witness borne to the Sovereignty of Jesus. That is why, even when he mentions features of Jesus' history, Paul always gives them their theological meaning.[1]

What is more, we may even ask ourselves whether Paul was not reacting against a tendency to attach too much importance to historical recollections of the life of Jesus. This, it seems, in the context where it appears, is the meaning of the famous passage which we quoted above: 'Even if we used to think of Christ in a human fashion, we do so no longer.' In other words, there was a danger of making Jesus into a great historical character, a figure in the past to whose teaching and example we must be brought back. And this is what He still is for many of our contemporaries. But this is exactly what Paul does *not* want, since for him Christ is a living reality. It is this Jesus who appeared to him at Damascus, who is in him and in whom he lives. Paul's personal gospel is to proclaim that Jesus lives.

This being admitted, the importance of the passages in which Paul does speak of the earthly life of Jesus is all the greater. If we take the Epistles, we find in them a certain number of references to the story of Jesus. First of all, the birth of Christ according to the flesh is stated in the Epistle to the Galatians: 'When the appointed time came, then God sent out his Son on a mission to us. He took birth from a woman, took birth as a subject of the law.'[2] These two phrases are important, the first indicating that Jesus was born of the Virgin Mary in the customary way, the second setting the birth of Jesus in the world of Judaism descended from the Old Testament.

[1] 1 Cor. 11 26.   [2] Gal. 4 4.

Another text refers to the birth of Christ, that of the Epistle to the Romans: 'Paul, a servant of Jesus Christ, called to be His apostle, and set apart to preach the gospel of God. That gospel, promised long ago by means of his prophets in the holy scriptures, tells us of his Son, descended, in respect of his human birth, from the line of David, but, in respect of the sanctified spirit that was his, marked out miraculously as the Son of God by his resurrection from the dead.'[1] Here it is the lineage of David which is stressed, and Paul clearly insists on this because of its Messianic significance. But he can only do this because it is for him a real historical fact. We always find the same principle at work: the selection of facts is not inspired by historical preoccupations, but it rests upon history.

The most important passages are connected with the events of the Passion, and first of all with the Last Supper. Here we have a key text: 'The tradition which I received from the Lord, and handed on to you, is that the Lord Jesus on the night when he was being betrayed, took bread, and gave thanks, and broke it, and said, Take, eat; this is my body, given up for you. Do this for a commemoration of me. And so with the cup, when supper was ended. This cup, he said, is the new testament, in my blood. Do this, whenever you drink it, for a commemoration of me.'[2] Here we have a very definite historical pointer, with details like 'when supper was ended.' St. Paul most certainly refers to the tradition of the primitive community.[3] We are undoubtedly concerned here with a key event from the dogmatic and liturgical point of view; and this explains the importance which St. Paul gives it. But the interesting

[1] Rom. 1 1-4.   [2] 1 Cor. 11 23-25.
[3] See Oscar Cullmann, *La Tradition*, pp. 15–19.

6

thing is that it shows how, when he wishes to do so, St. Paul gives us definite historical details.

On the Passion, Paul, in the First Epistle to Timothy, recalls that Christ 'bore witness to that great claim when he stood before Pontius Pilate.'[1] The First Epistle to the Thessalonians accuses the Jews of the death of Jesus: 'You were treated by your own fellow countrymen as those churches were treated by the Jews, the men who killed the Lord Jesus and the prophets.'[2] Usually Paul contents himself—but he does this frequently—with recalling the death of Jesus on the Cross. Thus in Philippians 2 [8]: 'He lowered his own dignity, accepted an obedience which brought him to death, death on a cross.' Or again: 'The chief message I handed on to you, as it was handed on to me, was that Christ, as the scriptures had foretold, died for our sins.'[3] It is worth noting that in these texts the emphasis is placed less upon the historical reality than upon the religious significance. And this already shows us that if Paul insists less upon the former, it is not that he is not familiar with it, but on the contrary that this reality was quite sufficiently known, and that the danger was in going no further and in saying that Jesus had died on the Cross like an ordinary man—and not that through this He had carried out God's plan.

The question is more complex when we come to consider the Gospels. Comparison of the first three among themselves shows that they use a collection of data which must have existed previously in a state which Dibelius calls that of 'little unities.' These consist of parables, accounts of miracles, practical teachings. But these little unities seem to have had as their context the life of the primitive community; they are preachings (Kerygma),

[1] 1 Tim. 6 [13].   [2] 1 Thess. 2 [14-15].   [3] 1 Cor. 15 [3].

7

catecheses, instructions. The Evangelists have arranged them in accordance with a historical scheme. But we notice, in the freedom with which they are arranged, that concern for historical accuracy was secondary with them, and that the Gospels in their turn are not 'Lives of Jesus' in the modern sense of the words, but writings intended perhaps for liturgical reading,[1] and whose very plan may well have been inspired by the requirements of this liturgical purpose.

All this research has enabled us little by little to sort out the 'literary forms' upon which the writings of the New Testament depend. The life of Christ is presented there in a stylized form. At first the authors were inspired to some degree by the literary forms of their times. Thus the accounts of the childhood of Jesus in St. Matthew seem very much in keeping with the Jewish accounts of the childhood of Moses, as Renée Bloch has shown.[2] Certain characteristics are emphasized: the persecutions which surround the child; the wisdom displayed by the youth; the long period of hidden life. In Luke, according to A. Laurentin,[3] they seem to depend upon another class of literature, the 'pesher,' of which already we find one form in the writings of Qumran. The events of the life of Jesus are here brought into line with the Old Testament prophecies which they fulfil; they are narrated with phrases borrowed from these; and it is sometimes difficult, in the case of certain details, to determine whether they come from historical data or from the pattern with which the story-teller is inspired.

This has already introduced us to a type of stylization which is not only the expression of literary customs, but

[1] See Harold Riesenfeld, *The Gospel Tradition and Its Beginnings*, pp. 21–23.
[2] 'Moïse dans la tradition rabbinique,' in *Moïse, l'homme de l'Alliance*, pp. 161–7.
[3] *Structure et Théologie de Luc* I–III, pp. 25–51.

which reveals a deeper intention. It is clear that, addressing Jewish, Aramaean or Hellenistic people, the Evangelists deliberately intended to set the life of Jesus in its relationship with the Old Testament. Matthew wishes to show us in Him a new Moses, and Luke the true Elias. The latter also retains episodes like the resurrection of the son of the widow of Naim, or that of the fire fallen from heaven, for which there were suitable parallels in the life of Elias.[1] One senses a process of editing which has been undertaken with definite preoccupations. The parallelism between the events in the life of Jesus in St. John's Gospel and the story of the Passover in Exodus is equally striking.[2]

Thus the juxtaposition of episodes in the Gospel which are reported to us by the Evangelists and certain accounts in the Old Testament or the Jewish *haggada* gives us the feeling that the latter have enabled us to sift out from among the data of the life of Christ those which lent themselves to parallel treatment, while the others were disregarded. Hence comes the feeling which we sometimes have of an almost paradigmatic character in the life of Christ in the Gospels, bringing it into line with some general system. But this does not mean that it has been built up in accordance with any such scheme, but that these systematic patterns have been applied to it in such a way that they draw forth from it a certain form, stressing the elements which concern the authors.

We shall have occasion to return to the fundamental meaning of the relationship which has already been established at the level of the New Testament between Christ and the people of Israel. For the moment, it shows

[1] See Jean Daniélou, *Advent*, 1950.
[2] See Harold Sahlin, *Zur Typologie des Johannesevangelium*, pp. 8–79.

us that the Gospels are not simply historical accounts intended to satisfy our curiosity, but testimonies designed to stir up faith. But this does not in the least mean that they are not based on a historical deposit. This extreme conclusion is one that we find in certain contemporary exegetes, such as Bultmann. The philological method ends by breaking down the image of Christ into heterogeneous elements, thereby obliterating it entirely. But the historical deposit of the Gospel is vindicated in opposition to any such literary decomposition.

How, then, are we to establish the historical consistency of the Gospel data concerning Jesus? Several types of consideration are brought into play here. The first is provided for us by the exegetes themselves. They find it necessary to take as a starting-point for their inquiry the Gospels simply as literary documents. But one of the results of their researches has been to show that these literary documents do not constitute the original element which brings us in contact with the life of Jesus. With the exception of St. John, the role of the Evangelists has been merely to put into writing, by arranging it in accordance with their respective standpoints, a deposit which preceded their activity. This deposit is the common tradition of the primitive community, of which they are simply the echo.

Now this strikingly modifies the terms of reference of the problem. For if there is one solid historical fact, it is the continuity of the primitive community with the person of Jesus—the framework of this community being the disciples of Jesus themselves. Peter, James and John belong at the same time to these two worlds. They play their part alike in the life of Jesus and in the primitive community. If, then, the basis of the evidence of the

Gospels, prior to their earliest editors, is the tradition of the primitive community, and if this tradition genuinely goes back to the Apostles, it becomes clear that the basis of the evidence of the Gospels springs from witnesses who shared the earthly life of Jesus. This, moreover, is the constantly repeated assertion of the Gospels and the Acts, that the witnesses to the faith of the community are also the witnesses to the earthly life of Jesus. They constitute the link between the Jesus of history and the Jesus of faith.

This enables us to grasp an essential rung in the ladder that connects us with the historical existence of Jesus. In fact, we need to remind ourselves that Christianity does not primarily rest upon the evidence of dead books, but of living men. In other words, the ultimate authority upon which the Christian faith rests is the evidence of the Apostles. It is this evidence which the Church transmits. She has always considered that this transmission was the essence of her mission. It is in relation to this evidence that she has distinguished what was authentic and what was not. The canonical Gospels are the written record of this evidence. And it is the Church which provides the basis of their authority by recognizing them as canonical, in the name of the apostolic authority which she continues.

If, then, it is upon the authority of the Apostles that our knowledge of the life of Jesus rests, we may say that our knowledge receives from that source an essential guarantee. By the same token we also have the explanation of the form in which these data of the life of Jesus are handed down to us. It is quite obvious that the Apostles must have emphasized not the anecdotal detail of the life of Jesus, which presented no difficulty for them, but its meaning for the faith which they themselves had discovered in the light of Pentecost, and to which they had to bear witness. In other words, far from stressing the human detail of the life of Jesus, it was necessary on the contrary to prevent people from resting content with mere human detail and to turn their eyes towards the mysterious content of the acts fulfilled in Jesus.

The Gospels thus present us with the life of Jesus as it was recaptured by the Apostles and the primitive community in the light of their preaching and teaching. The Gospels are the outward expression of what for the Apostles Jesus *was*. And ever since they have seemed to us to be just as important in relation to the story of Jesus as in relation to faith in Jesus. For the Apostles may be accurately described as the hinge between the two. And from that point the literary form of the Gospels becomes perfectly clear. It would be contrary to their purpose to rest content with being a mere biography of Jesus. But it would also be very unlikely that the historical data which they set before us should be without foundation, since these very data depend upon men who have themselves been their witnesses.

. . . . .

To these considerations, which arise from the very nature of the Gospels, we must add others derived from external evidence. This evidence does not bear directly on the person of Jesus Himself, and indeed it does not claim to do so. Christianity, in fact, only springs to life at the level of historiography as such, when it attains a sociological dimension. This is what we find at a very early date, in a Tacitus or a Pliny the Younger, when they show us the Christian community endowed with a sufficient solidarity for the power of Rome to take it into consideration. But from the point of view of history, the life of Jesus belonged to a private world which could not be appropriately written into a general history.

On the other hand, what contemporary evidence does enable us to verify is the historical and religious context in which the life of Christ, as described in the Gospels, was placed. This environment is that of Palestine in the first thirty years of our Era.

But can we arrive at such an understanding of this environment as to be able to compare it with the facts which the Gospels provide, in order to test their accuracy? Several classes of documents can help us here. On the one hand, we possess a Jewish commentary on the Law of Moses, the Talmud, edited at a later date, but made up of judgements of which a fair number go back to the rabbis of the time of Christ.

This rabbinic literature has been examined in a famous commentary by Billerbeck, who has brought together the various comparisons between the New Testament and Jewish tradition. A degree of uncertainty, however, results from the lateness of these traditions. The work, continued in our own day by David Daube,[1] Renée Bloch, W. D. Davis[2] and many others, is nevertheless developing very fruitfully. It does not bring us into contact with the events, but essentially with the customs and expressions of Judaism at the time of Christ, particularly as regards the interpretation of the Law by the scribes and Pharisees. Moreover, a considerable number of passages in the Gospel, particularly in the arguments in which Christ was involved, correspond very closely with what was current in contemporary Judaism.

A second class of documents comprises Jewish literature of the time of Christ, and is made up of what are called

---

[1] *The New Testament and Rabbinic Judaism*, 1956.   [2] *Paul and Rabbinic Judaism*, 1948.

the Apocryphal Books of the Old Testament. These curious works, The Book of Enoch, The Testaments of the Twelve Patriarchs, The Life of Adam and Eve, The Ascension of Moses, arise from a certain vision of the world which is termed apocalyptic. In essence it is composed of revelations made by God to His persecuted people to enable them to know the signs of the end, when God will intervene to destroy His enemies in no uncertain fashion. Thus it deals with a message of hope. Moreover, comparison with the teaching of Christ in the New Testament, especially the parables and certain discourses, shows that Christ uses the same thought-forms, and the ideas like 'revelation,' 'mystery' and 'the end' belong very much to this apocalyptic context.

It may be said, rather, that these documents only enable us to get a general impression of the environment of Christ, and one which is related especially to certain modes of thought. The Dead Sea discoveries have made considerable progress possible in this respect. In this case, what we are brought into contact with is a society in its wholeness, its organization, its accepted ideas and its history all at once, a society which corresponds historically and geographically with that in which the Gospels place Christ, and whose whole character convinces us that we are thus enabled to approach to the greatest possible extent the Judaism with which Christ was in direct contact. Let us give some examples of this.

John the Baptist was most probably in touch with the community at Qumran. He was baptizing only a short distance away. It is possible that his parents had entrusted him to the Essenes as a youth. His teaching has definite points of contact with the Dead Sea Scrolls. In both we find the idea that the last days have begun, that it is time to 'prepare in the desert the paths of the Lord,' that baptism of repentence is necessary for this preparation, that the judgement of this world is to come by fire. Nevertheless, it is not certain that John had been an Essene. On the other hand it is clear that, whether he came from Essenism or not, he had a prophetic vocation of his own, and was the founder of an original movement.[1]

When they list the great Jewish sects, the writers of the time mention the Essenes, the Pharisees and the Sadducees. Yet the first of these are never mentioned in the New Testament. This riddle has not yet found a satisfactory solution, but the most likely answer is that for Christ and His disciples the Essenes were not a sect, but formed part of 'the outcasts of Israel,' the 'true Israelites,' 'those who waited for the consolation of Israel.' This would seem to prove, then, that it is among the Essenes and their circle that Christ met one group of His disciples. It is clear, in any case, that He must have known of their existence.

The discovery of the Qumran Calendar perhaps enables us to solve one of the great riddles of the life of Christ— that of the day on which He celebrated the last Passover. St. John and the Synoptic Gospels are not in agreement with regard to this. On the other hand, an ancient tradition fixed the date as the evening of Tuesday in Holy Week. Now the Essenes had a calendar in which the Passover always fell on Wednesday, the 15th Nisan. It is possible, as Mlle. Jaubert suggests,[2] that Christ might have followed this calendar. Thus one difficulty in the Gospel account would be removed, for it is difficult to imagine that all the events of the Trial of Christ took place on the night of Thursday to Friday. In this case, they would have occupied

[1] See Jean Daniélou, *Les manuscrits de la Mer Morte et les origines du christianisme*, pp. 15–24.
[2] *La date de la dernière Cène*, 1957.

the three days between the Passover of the Essene calendar and the Passover of the official calendar.

The *Manual of Discipline* and a long fragment entitled 'Of the two columns' describe the meal of the Qumran community. This meal includes a blessing of the bread and a blessing of the wine at the beginning of the meal by the act of outstretching the hand. It seems clear that the meals which Christ took with the community of the Twelve had a similar ritual, and that it is in the course of the last of these meals that Christ instituted the Eucharist, transforming what was a simple blessing into a sacramental act, by which He changed the bread and wine into His body and blood.[1]

We encounter in the teaching of Jesus certain themes or phrases which reappear in the Qumran manuscripts. Thus we have the comparison of the community on the one hand, and the Church on the other, to a tree stretching out its branches over the world; thus, also, the use of the phrase 'bind and loose' to indicate the procedure with regard to sinners;[2] thus, also, the imagery of light and darkness to describe good and evil; thus, also, the term 'new covenant' and that of the Holy Spirit. One may certainly ask whether 'the teachings of Jesus and the beliefs of Qumran have something in common which is not found in other Jewish sources.'[3] At least this brings us into the midst of Jewish society at the beginning of our era.

The parallelism between the environment of the Gospels and that of Qumran is shown equally by their contrasts. The Essenes appear as scrupulous followers of legal observances. They went further in this respect than the

[1] K. G. Kuhn, 'Repas culturel essénien et cène chrétienne,' in *Les Manuscrits da la Mer Morte*, 1957, pp. 73–96.
[2] J. Schmitt, 'La discipline pénitentielle dans l'Église primitive à la lumière de Qumran,' ibid., pp. 98–100.
[3] Millar Burrows, *The Dead Sea Scrolls*, 1956.

Pharisees, as we know from a definite example, that of the beast fallen into a well on the Sabbath day, whose rescue the Pharisees permitted but the Essenes forbade. But the most striking characteristic of the behaviour of Christ, from the point of view of the Jews of the period, is the right which He assumed to break the Sabbath and the other observances, to the scandal of the Pharisees, the disciples of John, and therefore still more the Essenes.

This contrast appears particularly with regard to a most important point—concerning meals. The Essenes would never have agreed to eat with publicans and sinners; they would have thought that this polluted them; more than this, to be admitted to share their meal it was necessary first of all to pass through a two-year novitiate; and again, each meal had to be preceded by an ablution in the piscinas which have been discovered, and by a change of clothing. Now, as the protestant writer Lohmeyer has noticed,[1] nothing is more revolutionary in this sense, from the Essene point of view, than the fact that Christ ate with the unclean. And this action, as Lohmeyer well shows, had a Messianic significance. It was the expression of the breaking asunder of the narrowness of the Jewish community, even more constricted in the case of Qumran, and the call to all men to participate in the Messianic community.

Through these various approaches, to which many others could be added, and whatever discussion there may be on particular details, one thing at least is certain, that the environment which the Gospel describes, and therefore the person of Jesus who is its centre, seems to be part and parcel of a definite historical situation. It is this encounter with external documentary evidence that enables us to distinguish this historical side of the stylization

[1] 'Vom urchristlichen Abendmahl,' *Theol. Rundschau,* 1937, p. 276 f.

which the Gospel documents give it, and to see the real significance of this or that detail by putting them back into their context. From the religious as well as the political point of view, we discover a world which the Gospel records disclosed in a more stylized fashion, but which we now recognize to have been implied in its entirety.

The forces at work in this environment seem to be of a startling complexity. Palestine in the first century is a veritable melting-pot boiling over with all kinds of elements. Here we find the representatives of a strict, conservative Judaism in the circles of the high priests and leaders who were grouped together in the Sadducee party. The Pharisees, zealous defenders of the Law, are at pains to adapt it to present needs, and are developing a whole system of rabbinical casuistry. Among the Zealots, this concern for the Law takes the political form of a violent antagonism to the Roman occupation, and keeps the country in a continual ferment. At the opposite pole, the Herodian aristocracy represents a great cosmopolitan Judaism, open to Hellenistic culture and willing to expand with the Roman power.

On the fringes of these groups appear the Samaritans, combining their archaic Jewish foundation with a readiness to welcome the Oriental and Greek infiltrations which were an object of contempt to other Jews, a contempt whose echoes are heard several times in the Gospel. No doubt it is amongst them that the syncretism is elaborated which was later to result in *gnosis*, of which the Acts of the Apostles provides evidence in Simon Magus. Finally, closer to Jesus, the Essenes are the faithful heirs of the spirit of the Prophets, awaiting the deliverance which God alone shall bring, and separated from an official Judaism which seems to them to have sold its birthright.

If one reads the Gospel again in the light of all this, one sees how much Jesus is involved in this environment, and how He finds in it the context of His actions. He is in conflict with the hard conservatism of the Sadducees, who do not believe in the resurrection of the body or the existence of angels. On the other hand, He comes up against the hair-splitting of the Pharisees, who in their concern to settle the applications of the Law, throttle existence with regulations that destroy the spirit of the Law. He must resist the political power of the Zealots, who are trying to involve Him in their plan for a campaign against Rome. But He must also outwit the schemes of the Herodians, whose sympathy is hardly more than mere curiosity, vanishing over-night. He has compassion on the Samaritans, and it pleases Him to give them as an example of natural virtue. He draws His disciples from among the poor Essenes, but weans them from their narrow ideas of legal purity.

This 'belonging' of Christ to a definite historical environment is the most external approach to Him, and is precisely the one which was of no interest to the authors of the Gospels. That is why they are never concerned with it for its own sake. To reduce Christ to this level would be to see in Him nothing but the expression of the contemporary crisis of Judaism, nothing but the symbol of its contradictions. It would leave out of account not only the divine element revealed in Him, but even the qualities that properly belong to His true humanity. At the same time, this historical approach does provide a view of the reality of His humanity; it sets the Incarnation within the framework of history as historians see it, and forbids anyone to relegate Christ to the mere domain of faith. Thus history comes to add its unexpected evidence to that of the Apostles, in their capacity as witnesses to the earthly life of Jesus.

. . . . .

We have now examined several aspects of the question in hand, but we have not dealt with it. For the question is—to know what we can say of the personality and life of Jesus. And, strangely enough, it is precisely in the presence of this problem that, in the phrase of Vincent Taylor recalled by Père Léon-Dufour,[1] modern criticism is seized with a kind of 'intellectual paralysis.' It seems that here nobody likes to take a risk. If the assertion of the earthly life of Christ seems to be unquestioned, every attempt to penetrate into that earthly life seems to be forbidden by some unknown terror. Modern criticism speaks with less reluctance of the divinity of Christ than of His Humanity.

This attitude is explained by a number of legitimate refusals. There are images of Jesus which we can no longer tolerate. There is the archaeological reconstruction of the Galilean rabbi, which liberal Protestantism strove to create, and which was popularized by the lithographs of Burnand. There is the Jewish Jesus upheld by Sholem Asch and Jules Isaac, Jesus as seen by the Wandering Jew of Fley, which seems to be a moving witness borne to Jesus by the members of His race, but stops short at the threshold of that which surpasses race. There is the Socialist Jesus of Barbusse, the conscientious-objector Jesus of Van Lierde, the syncretist Jesus of Krishnamurti and Gandhi. There is Jesus the Teacher of Righteousness, whom Dupont-Sommer has subtly tried to introduce.[2]

It is true that in face of these images we can well under-

[1] 'Les Évangiles Synoptiques,' in Robert and Feuillet, *Introduction à la Bible*, II, p. 333.
[2] We might also speak of the 'Red' Jesus of Conrad Noel, the literary Jesus of Middleton Murry, the sensuous Jesus of D. H. Lawrence.—Trans.

stand Bultmann's disgust. For they seem to us to betray the essential thing, that liberating divine decision by which the coming of Christ bursts asunder the limitations of our existence. Everything that tends to reduce Christ, to force Him within the limits of human existence, is hostile to what is most precious and essential to us in Christianity. And we can quite understand that by a sort of extreme reaction we experience a kind of horror at psychologies and lives of Jesus.

It is also clear that this reaction runs the risk of going too far, and that it has already gone too far. If there was a danger of not taking seriously the divinity of Christ, there is also a danger of not taking seriously His humanity. For the mystery of Jesus is precisely the simultaneous affirmation of this twofold aspect. And strange to say, the greater paradox does not lie in affirming the divine aspect, but in affirming the human aspect. For the essential question that Christ presents is not that God should be God, that is to say, transcendent, but that God should be made man, that is, clothed in human nature. It was from this affirmation that the Gnostics withdrew when they declared that Christ had taken on a human appearance, when they saw in Him a phantom, an apparition. But this strikes at the very substance of the Christian faith. We are only saved if the Word of God really did assume human nature. And so this human nature is supremely important to us.

We can grasp the human nature of Christ through the Gospel at three levels of understanding. In its most external manifestation, it appears to us as revealing itself in the characteristic forms of its country and period. This is what we have called archaeological reconstruction; and indeed it provides its own share of truth. 'Jesus,' writes Père Léon-Dufour, 'an authentic Jew in His origin and behaviour, lived in Palestine . . .'; His doctrine is authentically traditional if we are to believe the judgement of the Jewish historian, J. Klausner: 'Jesus was a Jew and remained a Jew till his last breath.'[1] An entire picture of Christ follows from this connection. He spoke Aramaic. He lived in that Nazareth where Père de Foucauld went to find once more His bodily presence.

This historical setting may give us the feeling of that remoteness in time which affects everything historical. It is perhaps resistance to this view which makes us reluctant to consider Christ in His historical environment—it would relegate Him to a world of nostalgia, of an impossible return to an irrevocably vanished past. Now the assertion of faith is that He is the most vital reality of our own world. Yet despite this, His entry into history is one of the 'poles' of His plenitude. It gives Him roots in the fleshly race of Adam, in sonship of Abraham. It constitutes the paradox of the bursting-in of the divine act into the particularity of the historical event. And this paradox is essential to faith.

It is on this level that the comparison of Christ with the Teacher of Righteousness occurs, and the interesting analogies which this provides. For these analogies are real enough, and M. Dupont-Sommer has been right to emphasize them. 'The Galilean Master,' he writes, 'appears from many points of view as a reincarnation of the Teacher of Righteousness. Like the latter, He preached penitence, poverty, chastity, love of one's neighbour. Like him He commanded men to observe the Law of Moses, the whole Law, but the completed, perfect Law, according to His own revelations. Like him He was exposed to the hostility of the priests, to the party of the Sadducees. Like him

[1] loc. cit., p. 333.

22

He was condemned and punished.'[1] I omit from this comparison some features in which by a reverse process the author describes the Teacher of Righteousness with Jesus' own characteristics. He has himself already emphasized the essential differences.

The interest of this comparison of Jesus with the Teacher of Righteousness is precisely that, by giving us a point of reference in the very society in which He lived, it makes it possible for us to distinguish in Jesus what He has in common with a great religious personality of His time and setting, and what is absolutely His own. But this does not prevent us from seeing all that He provides in other respects, namely the expression of His time and something which serves as the seal of the truth of His earthly life.

But if the humanity of Jesus is thus written into the texture of a period and a country, it is clear, too, that on the very level of this texture His humanity overflows it to be reunited with the whole of mankind. If Christ is descended from the race of Abraham, He has been rejected by that race, and for the very reason that He refused to let His destiny be enclosed within the destiny of that race. He belongs to all men, and He is reunited with the universal experience of man at its very core. And there, without question, lies one of the most arresting peculiarities we find in Him. There are plenty of men who do not believe in Christ. But there are few men who do not love Him. And in this case, whether it is Gandhi, or Barbusse, they are affirming something of the truth when they acknowledge that they have been conquered by Him.

This is important, first of all, inasmuch as Christ appears as having expressed the drama of the human condition in an exemplary form. The words of Pilate: 'Behold the

[1] *Aperçus preliminaires sur les manuscrits de la Mer Morte*, p. 121.

man,' retain a lasting value. St. Irenaeus has already noted that Christ had 'recapitulated' man. It is to this aspect that the philosophers are drawn. For Hegel, Christ represents the absolute Idea of man. His Passion takes on a universal character as the expression of the victory of love over egoism. But although we must admit that this rational simplification misses the essential character of Christ, it nevertheless expresses something genuine. There is in the manhood of Christ something to which every man feels himself related in a brotherly manner.

Not only does Christ appear to us as having shared our human condition, but we see Him holding fast to that condition and ratifying it to some extent by His attitude to it. This is what I mean. We encounter, in the setting to which Christ belonged, many currents that suggest a condemnation of man's condition, especially of his bodily life. The Platonists saw in the body a prison from which death would finally liberate the soul. Encratism, which certainly has Jewish roots,[1] condemned some forms of food, saw in sexual life as such an evil reality. Soon the Gnostics were to issue a wholesale condemnation of the entire creation. But in Christ's behaviour there is nothing like this. He seems, with regard to the creation, to be filled with awe as in the presence of God's handiwork. One does not feel in Him any contempt for the lowly realities of human existence. He makes use of the good things of the body, and the Gospel emphasizes that He does not follow the asceticism of a John the Baptist. He shares the feelings of the human heart—He weeps at the death of his friend Lazarus, He is shaken with anger at the sight of the hypocritical Pharisees, He experiences before His own death the spontaneous horror which it inspires in the flesh.

[1] See Erik Peterson, *Frühkirche, Judentum und Gnosis*, pp. 183-235.

There is nothing in Him of the harsh attitude of a Stoic morality which consists in a kind of insensibility which aims at an attitude of detachment towards suffering, neither is there anything to indicate complicity with suffering. But there is an extraordinary normality in His human reactions.

And yet with regard to these human realities, towards which one feels in Him no attitude of depreciation, Jesus shows at the same time a sovereign independence. The Gospel, in this sense, is filled with an extraordinary breath of freedom. To tell the truth, this freedom is another form of dependence. It means that for Christ the will of God is the only chain by which He is bound. Thereafter He does not recognize the right of any creature to be an obstacle to this faithfulness to the divine will. He does not despise the family, but He recognizes its limitations: 'Could you not tell that I must needs be in the things which are my Father's?' He weeps over Jerusalem, His homeland, but He refuses to be dominated by the service of the earthly city. This unique attitude, which is that of the Sermon on the Mount, expresses a new ethic which has not ceased to resound through human history, and of which the ideologies of freedom and the person remain with us to-day as secularized 'left-overs.'

This universality of the manhood of Christ finds expression, in the last place, in the bursting asunder of the religious and national particularisms which were a feature of the tradition of Israel. Here once again our statement rests on the most reliable historical context. Judaism of the time of Christ was characterized by a particularism which was especially rigorous among the Essenes, who constituted a community of the pure, separated from pagan societies and avoiding all contact with them. The act of Christ in eating with publicans and sinners appears as a revolutionary and strictly Messianic act, signifying that henceforth the Kingdom of God is open to all. This declaration of the equal value of all human persons is a typical characteristic of Christ's conduct.

Christ, moreover, refuses to ally Himself with the nationalism of the Zealots. He declares in this way that henceforth a new age has opened in which, as Paul says, there is 'neither Jew nor Greek.' The Incarnation of Christ is here the expression of a charity which engulfs the whole of humanity. And the command in the Sermon on the Mount, 'Love your enemies,' is ever its seal. That is to say that all sociological barriers are broken down, or rather that sociological barriers correspond to a human order which has its own proper place, but that beyond that order there is another order, where all men now are members of but one single society, so that it is in the light of this new order that the qualities of the old order are placed.

Thus the manhood of Jesus appears to us through the New Testament as recapitulating man on his various levels in His historical uniqueness, in His human universality. Finally, we must add this: human nature appears to us in Christ as realizing an unsurpassable perfection of human nature. This at the outset might well put us on our guard. The portrait of Jesus is so ideal that we might ask whether, to be quite accurate, it is not more of an ideal than a reality. But this ideal character is not accurately expressed through abstract rules. Nothing is more concrete than the Gospel, nor further removed from those moral allegories which it pleased the authors of the time to write. Even in someone like Philo of Alexandria, a contemporary of Christ, the figures of the Old Testament, so concrete in the Bible, become the νόμος ἔμψυχος, the ideal expression of the Law.

And the hagiographies, in which concrete realities melt away, arouse our justifiable mistrust.

But the Gospel confronts us with something quite different. It is through His conduct that Christ appears to us as the very realization of man in God's design, as the religious summit of humanity. In this respect, the remarks of Duméry are exactly right; and so is Pascal's saying: 'We can only know ourselves through Jesus Christ.' It is in Him that the true face of man's destiny, the mystery of man's self-significance, which all the introspection in the world is powerless to grasp, is revealed. Genesis, by saying that God created man in His own image, showed at one stroke man's relation to the world and his relation to God, his transcendence with regard to the world, his total dependence with regard to God. In Jesus, it is this image of God which is brought to fulfilment. The holiness of His manhood is the expression at once of this sovereign freedom with regard to the world and this absolute recognition of the sovereignty of God.

This holiness of Christ's humanity is expressed by His complete separation from all sin. And here we come upon a fact of special importance. For sin is normally part of the present condition of man, and the fact of acknowledging himself to be a sinner normally appears even as the mark of spiritual authenticity. Christ Himself has told us that no man is sinless. The comparison with the Teacher of Righteousness is relevant here. One of his most wonderful characteristics is the knowledge he has of being a sinner. In this context the word of Christ—'Can any of you convict me of sin?'—assumes a unique significance. Either it is an inadmissible claim—in which case we would be compelled to say that Christ is not a holy person. And who would dare to say that? Or else it must be acknowledged that He is speaking the truth—in which case His very behaviour brings it home to us that the features of His humanity cannot be explained simply in terms of His humanity, and when we come to the highest points of His humanity we necessarily encounter something quite different from itself. It is just on that threshold that we come to the end of this chapter.

.   .   .   .   .

We have approached Christ through the ordinary channels by which every man can approach Him, by the reading of the Gospel. We have been convinced, by this contact, of the historical and human truth of Jesus. This truth constitutes evidence which must be faced by every well-informed mind acting in good faith. And justifiable discussion is able to be brought to bear upon what the Gospels enable us to grasp of the life and personality of Jesus, but not upon the fact that they enable us to grasp that life and personality in their essential features. At the same time as we grasped this Manhood of Jesus, we gave some account of what was artificial about it, and halted our inquiries there. For the documents which set the humanity of Christ before us represent it only as the humanity of the Son of God. We have felt that, the moment we tried to isolate it from this connection, in some sense it vanished amid the anaemic pictures which are presented by the rationalist historians. Thus it seemed clear to us, at one and the same time, that the Manhood was real—and we must therefore try to clarify certain aspects of it—and that we could only understand it within the entire context of what is presented by the totality of Christ. This is the next subject of our inquiry.

BIBLIOGRAPHY

Introduction à la Bible, sous la direction de A. Robert et A. Feuillet, Tome II, *Le Nouveau Testament*, Paris, 1959.

E. HOSKYNS and N. DAVEY, *The Riddle of the New Testament*, London, 1931.

H. RIESENFELD, *The Gospel Tradition and its Beginnings*, London, 1957.

J. DANIÉLOU, *Les Manuscrits de la Mer morte et les origines du christianisme*, Paris, 1958.

The Scrolls and the New Testament, ed. Krister Stendahl, London, 1958.

F. M. BRAUN, *Jean le Théologien et son Évangile dans l'Église ancienne*, Paris, 1959.

CHAPTER II

GOD MADE MAN

THE confession of the Divinity of Christ is the essential object of faith, which, St. Paul tells us, consists in recognizing the identity of Jesus of Nazareth with the creative Word. It is an astonishing assertion, and we are quite entitled to examine its basis and to ask ourselves whether the Gospel actually requires us to accept it. Some critics, indeed, maintain that the deification of Christ was the work of the primitive community and did not correspond to what we can discover of Jesus Himself. And it goes without saying that if this divinity was only the subject of certain affirmations, we might always suspect such passages of having been added or recast for apologetic purposes.

However, it is not these explicit statements, of which in any case there are few in the Synoptic Gospels, that we shall first consider. It is the behaviour of Christ Himself, in His own actions and the reactions which they arouse, that will be our concern. This constitutes the very pattern of His public life, and gives rise to a drama which reaches its climax in His trial and death. What we wish to show is that this pattern of the life of Christ, and in particular His trial and death, cannot be explained except by the fact that He claimed divine authority. One might challenge His right to do this, and indeed this is the question that the High Priests raised. From the Jewish point of view, it was quite legitimate to condemn Him as a blasphemer. But what cannot be challenged, without bringing into question not only the isolated sayings but the whole range of the events of His life and death, is that He did claim that authority.

So it is first of all the conduct of Christ during His earthly life that we shall examine. Only after that shall we take into account two other classes of data which may support our conclusions. The first is that of the actual words of Christ and the evidence which He provided of Himself. It amounts to a commentary by Christ on His own behaviour. The second class of data is the conception which was formed of Him by His first disciples and the early Christian community. Their evidence is all the more valuable since, having known Christ during His earthly life, they realized to the full the startling quality of His claim to Divinity. Above all we must add that, being Jews, they had a profound horror of any divinization of man, and that if they worshipped Jesus as being Himself the Lord, it was just because they were compelled to this belief by a certainty from which they found it impossible to withdraw, and not in the least because they were forced by their religious bent to accept it.

. . . . . .

We have first to review the various parts of the Gospel in which we see Christ claiming an authority that belongs to God alone. The first is His attitude to the Law. In the Sermon on the Mount we read these words: 'You have heard it was said to the men of old, Thou shalt do no murder. . . . But I tell you that any man who is angry with his brother must answer for it before the Court of justice.'[1] The passage refers to Exodus 20 [13], that is, to the Law given by Yahweh to Moses on Sinai. Jesus takes up the same theme with regard to various articles of the Law. Jesus thus acknowledges that He has the right to modify what was established by Yahweh Himself. But this amounts to a claim on Jesus' behalf that He is the equal

[1] St. Matt. 5 [21-22].

of Yahweh. Indeed, only He who established the Law can modify the Law. I remember hearing a rabbi say: 'Well, Father, what we cannot approve of in Christ is that He meddled with the Law. For the Law was established by God, and God alone can alter it.' This is profoundly true. To alter the Law is equivalent to Jesus' proclaiming Himself the Son of God.

One aspect of the behaviour of Christ, which is an example of His general attitude to the Law, but which has a quite special importance, is His attitude to the Sabbath. The text in Matthew is particularly significant. The disciples were plucking the ears of corn on the Sabbath day. The Pharisees were shocked at this. Jesus then replies with this startling phrase: 'The Son of Man has even the sabbath at his disposal.'[1] It is very interesting to notice the passages in the Gospel in which Jesus is said to have scandalized the Jews, for they emphasize Jesus' specific intentions. Thus the Pharisees were horrified when Jesus ate with publicans and sinners; and it is true that according to the Law this would make Him legally unclean. It is sufficient to recall the incident at Antioch when, for fear of the Jewish Christians, Peter refuses to eat with Christians of pagan origin, for us to realize how deep-seated was this aversion. The Essenes carried it to extremes, requiring two years of purification before admission could be granted to their sacred meal. By breaking these regulations Jesus shows, as Yves de Montcheuil has clearly seen,[2] that the barriers presented by the Law are abolished, that the only condition for anyone to be admitted to communion with God is henceforth to be faith in His Person.

It is the same with regard to the Sabbath, which was

[1] St. Matt. 12 8.
[2] 'La signification eschatologique du repas eucharistique.' *RSR*, 1936, pp. 5 et seq.

indeed divinely instituted, and was one of the holiest of such institutions. The first chapter of Genesis shows it to be written into the very structure of creation itself. The Pharisees had therefore every right to be scandalized at the freedom of Christ's attitude with regard to the Sabbath. Their opposition does not arise' from any hostility based on reasons of human jealousy. It belongs strictly to the religious order. It shows their zeal for the Law established by God. But at the same time it shows too that Christ's action has a religious meaning. It bears witness to the fact that He assumes the right to modify what God has established. 'The Son of Man has even the sabbath at his disposal.' The Pharisees see the point of His action. And in this respect their hostility is capital evidence of the fact that Christ claimed divine prerogatives, for it is the evidence of opponents—and it is their opposition that comprises the centre of the public life of Christ.

The meaning of Jesus' attitude to the Sabbath is made equally explicit in the Gospel according to St. John. It was a question of healing the paralytic at Bethesda on the Sabbath day. But he answered them: 'My Father has never ceased working, and I too must be at work. This made the Jews more determined than ever to make away with Him, that he not only broke the Sabbath, but spoke of God as his own Father, by treating himself as equal to God.'[1] These last words are particularly decisive. The deep-seated reason for the Jews' hostility to Jesus was the fact that He made Himself 'equal with God.' This is truly the supreme blasphemy, man's claim to be the equal of the transcendent God.

This brings us to the heart of the question. The greatest of sins for the Jews was man's claim to be as God: *Eritis*

[1] St. John 5 17-18.

sicut dei. In the midst of an idolatrous world, the people of Israel were the jealous guardians of the transcendence of God. Their mission is to denounce all forms of idolatry. Accordingly it is in the name of what they hold to be most essential that they oppose Jesus when He claims His divine authority. This puts the problem on its appropriate level and gives the drama of the life of Christ its exemplary value. We have irrefutable evidence that Christ was considered by the Jews to have claimed divine prerogatives. It is with this that history confronts us. The question which then arises is whether He had the right to make this claim. The drama of Israel is that, faced with the Christ, it had no choice but to adore Him or crucify Him. And to crucify Him was yet to bear witness that He had declared Himself to be the Son of God.

We shall notice, too, that if Christ breaks the Sabbath, it is not to destroy it, but to fulfil it. For to Him the Law is holy, because it was given by His Father. Not a jot shall pass away. So it is not to abolish it that He has come. But the Law corresponded to a moment in the work of God. As soon as that for which the Law was a preparation has arrived, the Law becomes superfluous. Now, Jesus announces that He is this fulfilment. That is to say, He claims not only to be He who gives the new Law, but to be that Law itself, which is His Person. He is the Word of God no longer spoken only to the Prophet, but appearing in His personal substance. He is not only the giver of the Sabbath, He is the Sabbath of the New Covenant, the 'rest' (ἀνάπαυσις) for your souls which He proclaims in the same context as that of the breaking of the Sabbath.[1]

This appears also in another theme, that of the Temple. The Temple is, with the Law, God's great gift to Israel.

[1] St. Matt. 11 29.

It is, in fact, the expression of the Shekinah, of the Presence of God in the midst of His people, a pre-eminent work of God. Now in the Gospel we see Jesus putting Himself side by side with the Temple. In the episode of the money-changers cast out of the Temple, He first reveals Himself as being at home in the House of God. The Jews are astonished at this. Christ then begins to act by saying, 'Destroy this temple, and in three days I will raise it up again.'[1] And John's comment leaves no doubt as to the meaning of this saying: 'But the Temple he was speaking of was his own body.'[2] Elsewhere we have a saying of Jesus Himself which is equally explicit: 'There is one standing here who is greater than the Temple.'[3]

The Temple is the place where Yahweh's Presence is. When Jesus declares by His words and reveals by His actions that He is greater than the Temple, He is clearly referring to the essential feature of the Temple—the Presence of God—and declares that henceforth, as Yahweh dwelt in the Temple of the Old Testament, so it is He who is the New Temple, one who is at the same time the Presence and the place of the Presence, God present among men in a more excellent manner in His manhood. This is very much how the Evangelists were to understand the matter when they show us, as in John, the Word of God establishing His Presence in Jesus through the Incarnation, or, as in the Synoptics, the veil of the Temple being rent at the time of the Passion, to show that the divine Presence is henceforth in Jesus.

Now we have a specially remarkable proof of the fact that the attitude of Jesus with regard to the Temple was, on His part, truly the assertion of His divinity. This is the saying of Jesus to the Pharisees which is to be the

[1] St. John 2 19.   [2] St. John 2 21.   [3] St. Matt. 12 6.

evidence reserved for the trial of Jesus, as a basis for the accusation of blasphemy.[1] In these solemn circumstances, Christ thus acknowledged that the statement which He had made had indeed the bearing which the Sanhedrin had given it. The sentence brought against Him is the official evidence, given in public proceedings, of the assertion of His divinity by Jesus Himself. We say no more for the present. The sentence which was delivered against Christ does not prove that He was God. But it surely proves that He claimed to be God, and it eliminates entirely any picture of Christ which would make Him merely a prophet. Such a Jesus as this has only existed in the critics' imagination. The only Jesus who really existed is He who represented Himself as the Son of God, and was put to death for that by a legal judgement. For if the Jews did not believe in Him, they were obliged according to the Law to condemn him: 'By our Law he ought to die, for pretending to be the Son of God.'[2]

We have not, however, reached the end of this series of statements. One of the ways in which Christ claims divine power is in the right to forgive sins. The report of the healing of the sick of the palsy is especially worth noticing in this respect: 'And Jesus, seeing their faith, said to the palsied man, Son, thy sins are forgiven. But there were some of the scribes sitting there, who reasoned in their minds, Why does he speak so? He is talking blasphemously. Who can forgive sins but God, and God only?'[3] Here we encounter once more the accusation of blasphemy, and the scribes are quite right to prefer this charge. For, as they have good reason to believe, only God can forgive sins. This means, then, that by claiming to forgive sins Jesus arrogates to Himself the very power of

[1] St. Matt. 6 61-65.   [2] St. John 19 7.   [3] St. Mark 2 5-7.

36

God. This is a new piece of evidence which His enemies bring forward against Jesus' assertion of His divinity.

It is true, indeed, that forgiveness of sins is a divine prerogative. The Old Testament bears witness: 'It is I, I, the Lord; no other can bring deliverance.'[1] Sin, in the theological sense of the word, is a state of separation from God, a spiritual death, a state over which man has no control. And this is just what men find it, an inexorable reality which brings into human life a rift that nothing can repair, which strikes at man's spiritual vitality, and which casts a veil of sadness over all existence. Sin excludes man from Paradise, from being in harmony with all things—a harmony outside the possibility of which everything becomes pointless. Sin, too, is so congenital to man that modern philosophers have reached the point of regarding it as his essence, seeing failure and anguish as the very basis of existence. Only the power of God can penetrate to the radical evil, the root of evil, which is within man but beyond his control. Only He can open the gates of Paradise once more to the transgressor. Only He can heal the sores of wounded Adam, abandoned by the priests and scribes.

In the scene at Capharnaum Christ not only forgives sins, He also heals bodies. Thus He declares that He has at the same time power over spiritual and corporeal death. This is a fresh statement of His divine power. It is set forth in all its fullness in the episode which occupies a leading place in the life of Christ, for it marks the moment when the hostility of the Jews becomes militant, and it inaugurates the drama which is to reach its climax in the Passion. It is impossible, therefore, to question that it belongs to the very texture of the Gospel; otherwise it

[1] Isa. 43 [11].

37

would be necessary to question that texture itself, to doubt the historicity of Jesus. And we have seen that this is scientifically untenable. The raising of Lazarus, is, then, one of the turning points of the Gospel. It belongs to the pattern of the life of Jesus in the anecdotal sense of the word. At the same time it causes the intervention of a strictly divine action into the pattern of phenomena. In raising Lazarus, Jesus reveals the fact that He is master of life and death. But this again is strictly a divine prerogative; it goes far beyond the possibilities that are proper to man, and is essentially, and not only through ignorance, something beyond the capabilities of man.

Here again Jesus continues the action of Yahweh in the Old Testament. It is Yahweh who is the Lord of life no less than death,[1] whilst Jesus tells Martha in the episode of the raising of Lazarus: 'I am the resurrection, and the life; he who believes in me, though he is dead, will live on.'[2] We are confronted here by that divine 'I' who claims the power of life and death as belonging to His own power and not as derived from another. Peter, too, raises from the dead, but he does it in the name of the Lord Jesus. Jesus raises Lazarus in His own name. This is the important thing to notice when we are discussing in what sense the attitude of Jesus is to be regarded as the claiming of a strictly divine character for His own person.

We shall notice, indeed, the unique tone which appears in Jesus' utterances, and which so much affected His contemporaries. 'Nobody has ever spoken as this man speaks'[3] said the Jews; and again: 'He taught them, not like the Scribes, but like one who had authority.'[4] In fact, there is in the words of Christ a unique quality that strikes us even

---

[1] Cp. Isa. 45 [7].   [2] St. John 11 [25].   [3] St. John 7 [46].   [4] St. Matt. 7 [29].

before we have fathomed its character. It is quite different from that of the Old Testament Prophets. These latter pass on a message which they have received: 'The Word of Jehovah was spoken to me in these terms.' This is also the tone which Mohammed was to adopt later on: he is the Prophet entrusted with the communication of the oracles of God. But Jesus speaks in quite another manner. He does not refer to an authority other than His own. He speaks of His own authority. He claims the right to demand that absolute and unconditional obedience which is only due to God Himself.

Here comparison with the Old Testament is instructive. Christ's mode of expression certainly does not correspond to that of the Prophets. They never use the words 'I say unto you,' but 'This is what God says to you.' In fact, the utterance of Jesus in the New Testament has continuity with the speech of Yahweh in the Old Testament. As K. L. Schmidt and others following him have shown,[1] the 'I' of Jesus is the 'I' of Yahweh, the expression of the statement of absolutely sovereign divine personality. The equivalent to Jesus' manner of speech is to be found in passages like this, 'The Lord has pronounced it; the Lord who made the heavens. . . . It is the Lord that speaks, there is no other rival to me, it was not in secret, not in some dark recess of the earth. . . . I am the Lord, faithful to my promises, truthful in all I proclaim.'[2] It will be noticed that Jesus takes up this very passage to apply it to Himself: 'I have spoken openly before the world. Nothing that I have said was said in secret.'[3] Similarly in another passage Yahweh says: 'It is I, the Lord thy God, that hold

---

[1] K. L. Schmidt, *Le problème du christianisme primitif*, pp. 35-44. C. H. Dodd, *The Interpretation of the Fourth Gospel*, p. 168.
[2] Isa. 45 18-19.   [3] St. John 18 20.

thee by the hand and whisper to thee. Do not be afraid.'[1]
This recalls Mark 6 [50]: 'It is myself; do not be afraid.'

These statements of Jesus are concerned with different
objects. On the one hand they relate to manifestations of
power. Thus Jesus casts out the devil from the epileptic
child: 'It is I that command thee.'[2] The first person is
similarly used in the sentence: 'I can tell that power has
gone out from me,'[3] with its relation to the δύναμις.
Elsewhere it is a question of sending out the Apostles:
'I am sending prophets.'[4] Elsewhere again, it is a question
of teachings: 'But I tell you.'[5] In St. John's Gospel the
formula is more complete: 'Believe me when I tell you this.'[6]

More important still are the passages where Christ names
Himself absolutely as 'I' with the personal character and
sovereign freedom which characterize the revelation of
the God of Exodus: 'I am the God who is.' So in the verse
of St. John: 'When you have lifted up the Son of Man, you
will recognize that it is myself.'[7] We find several of these
Ego Sum passages with this same absolute character. In
the meeting with the Samaritan woman we find it again:
'I, who speak to thee, am the Christ.'[8] And the episode of
the man that was born blind provides an equivalent.[9] It
appears again later: 'that ye may believe that it is myself.'[10]
Sometimes the expression is accompanied by an image: 'It is
I who am the bread of life. . . . I am the way, I am truth
and life. . . . I am the resurrection and life.'

It may be objected that Christ attributes to the Father
who is in heaven the powers which the Old Testament
acknowledges in Yahweh.[11] And it is true that this is
mysterious. Jesus not only claims an authority equal to

[1] Isa. 41 [13].   [2] St. Mark 9 [24].   [3] St Luke 8 [46].
[4] St. Matt. 23 [34].   [5] St. Matt. 5, [22, 28, 34, 39].   [6] St. John 8 [51] etc.
[7] St. John 8 [28].   [8] St. John 4 [26].   [9] St. John 9 [37].
[10] St. John 13 [19].   [11] St. Matt. 5 [45].

that of Yahweh; He announces that He possesses this authority in His own right. In other respects, nevertheless, He acknowledges that His authority belongs to the Father. Thus this authority belongs at once to the Father and to Him. But it is precisely this that reveals in the very action of Jesus, not merely the claim to divine authority, but also the assertion that He is a divine Person distinct from the Father. Thus we are shown the concrete character of the Trinity in the Gospel. It is disclosed by the attitudes of Christ. It demonstrates modes of action through which modes of being are revealed. And these modes of action are all tied up with events whose historical texture is unquestionable. This it is in which the life of Christ necessarily involves the mystery of Christ.

Certainly the collection of passages which we have just studied presents a unique problem. It seems to be undeniable from a historical point of view that Jesus claimed divine authority. Nor is it a mere passing phrase or any isolated act, but His whole bearing that forces us to this conclusion. This apart, nothing can any longer be explained, neither the opposition which He encountered, nor the accusation of blasphemy, nor His trial, nor His death. He was a 'dilemma.' He drove the men in the midst of whom He lived to a position from which there was no escape. Thenceforward, on the question of whether He was what He insisted He was, only two attitudes were possible—either to condemn Him as a blasphemer, or to worship Him as the Son of God. No neutrality was possible. And we must add that Christ has not ceased to present this question to every man, that He continues to present a challenge to every age.

There are two possible answers to the question. Either Christ is an impostor, clever or foolish, who thought he was God or wished to pass as such. This kind of imposture is possible; there have been examples of it. But they always arise from a wretched type of humanity, from cynics or unbalanced people, whereas all men are agreed, and that without exception, in recognizing Christ at the very least as one of the most outstanding representatives of mankind, one of the highest religious peaks to which it has attained. One can only admire His astonishing wisdom, His abounding goodness, the clearness of His mind. Indeed, this is something that Hindus and Jews, Muslims and atheists, unanimously recognize. There are few men who do not love Jesus. How, then, could we tolerate the idea that this same man could have been an impostor? If it is not possible to have confidence in Christ, confidence is no longer possible in anything whatever. There is no longer any difference between good and evil. Nothing any longer makes sense. There is a contradiction in loving Jesus and not believing in Jesus, in seeing Him as the summit of mankind and not believing what He says.

The value of evidence, as Jean Guitton has clearly shown, is bound up with the value of the witness. There are people—we all know them—whom one knows one can trust. Our inability to trust in this case springs from confusion and not from clearness of mind. For Christ fulfils to the highest degree the conditions of a trustworthy witness. If what He said did not seem extraordinary, if, above all, what He said did not confront us with a choice which involves our whole life, there would not be the least hesitation with regard to the trust which His words deserve. Granted this, it must be recognized that in spite of the humanly improbable character of what He said, it seems strictly correct, with full intellectual rigour and without any concession to personal prejudices—or rather in spite of all objections and hesitations—to believe that Christ told the truth, and that the impossible is a fact. This is what many of the disciples said after the words of Christ: 'You can have no life in yourselves, unless you eat the flesh of the Son of Man, and drink His blood.' Truly 'this is a strange talk, who can be expected to listen to it?' But, as Peter says: 'Lord, to whom should we go? Thy words are the words of eternal life.'[1]

.   .   .   .   .

So far we have considered Christ's general attitude. Now we can turn to examine His words and what He tells us of Himself. We shall deal particularly with what St. John tells us of the matter. This evidence has a quite special value, for St. John is the Beloved Disciple who not only knew Christ, but lived in closer intimacy with Him than any other. He is, in this sense, a witness of the highest quality to the life of Christ, and he claims this character on several occasions: 'He who saw it has borne his witness; and his witness is worthy of trust.'[2] Or again: 'Our message concerns that Word, who is life; what he was from the first, what we have heard about him, what our own eyes have seen of him, what it was that met our gaze, and the touch of our hands. Yes, life dawned; and it is as eye-witnesses that we give you news of that life.'[3]

At the same time John is the Evangelist who is most explicit about the Divinity of Jesus. In this Gospel, Christ speaks of His relationship with the Father in a manner which leaves no doubt as to His Divinity. John has preserved these words of Jesus in his memory. The phrasing that he gives them may reflect his own linguistic customs, but the authenticity of their content cannot be denied. They constitute a unified statement by Jesus about

---

[1] St. John 6 [54, 61, 69]   [2] St. John 19 [35].   [3] St. John I [1-2].

Himself which at once confirms and completes what His behaviour revealed in a concrete fashion. They form a kind of commentary upon it. The unique character of this revelation by Christ Himself of His Divinity enables us to find in St. John the privileged expression of the proof of the Divinity of Christ at the level not of actions, but of words.

First we may refer to the passages in which Christ announces that He belongs to a world other than that of the creation: 'He who comes from above is above all men's reach.'[1] Christ emphasizes here that His origin is not earthly. He comes from God. And indeed it is striking that we do not feel that He is at any distance from the world of God. He is on the same level as it. Comparison with the Teacher of Righteousness is instructive here. The Teacher of Righteousness has the sense of his nothingness before the sovereign Lord. Christ never seems to adopt this attitude. And it is His perfect connaturality with God that is proved by passages like the one we have quoted. John in turn gives the definitive formulation of this statement when he writes in his Prologue: 'God had the Word abiding with him, and the Word was God.'

His belonging to the divine implies that in fact Christ existed before His earthly birth. It is this statement that we find in an amazing passage. Addressing the Jews, Christ says: 'As for your father Abraham, his heart was proud to see the day of my coming; he saw, and rejoiced to see it.' Then the Jews asked Him, 'Hast thou seen Abraham, thou, who art not yet fifty years old?' And Jesus said to them, 'Believe me, before ever Abraham came to be, I am.'[2] Here the entire significance of the statement arises from its relationship with the concrete data of chronology.

---

[1] St. John 3 31. See also 8 21.   [2] St. John 8 56-58.

The Jews rightly objected that in order to have known Abraham, Jesus would have had to be hundreds of years old. But in His divine Person, Jesus does not belong to the time of this world. And in His eternal pre-existence He comes before all times and is contemporary with all times. Words like these open an abyss in the pattern of Jesus' life, making transparent for a moment the sphere to which He does not cease to belong.

The divine origin of Christ explains the meaning of His work. He 'came down from heaven' to fulfil the work which His Father entrusted to Him; and this work is to 'keep without loss, and raise up at the last day, all he has entrusted to me.'[1] In so far as Christianity can be described as faith in an act of God coming down to men, we find here the very substance of it. It is not necessary to be a Christian to believe in the existence of a God. And religion in its essence is precisely man's groping search for God. But this search can have no end. For between transcendent God and created man there is an unbridgeable gulf. 'No man has ever seen God.' That gulf cannot be crossed, only God can cross it. And the Christian claim is precisely that the gulf has been crossed. Christ is the occasion. He is God's search for man, which alone can end man's search for God. He is God drawing near to man in order that man may draw near to God.

In this perspective other passages must be examined afresh: 'It was from the Father I came out, when I entered the world, and now I am leaving the world, and going on my Way to the Father.'[2] The twofold movement which constitutes the mystery of Christ is clearly stated here. He is first of all the Son of God coming into the world. This is the very act of the divine *agape*, the movement of

[1] St. John 6 [39].   [2] St. John 16 [28].

God seeking for man.[1] But God only seeks for man in order to lead man to God, for the Son of God raises the manhood, which He took at the Incarnation above itself, and brings it into the House of God, into the unfathomable region of the Trinity. He is thus the bridge across the gulf, the path of man to God. 'I am the way; I am truth and life: nobody can come to the Father, except through me.'[2] And indeed, if 'no man has ever seen God, his only-begotten Son, who abides in the bosom of the Father, has himself become our Interpreter.'[3]

The emphasis in all this is placed upon the absolute necessity of the coming of God to man in order to give man access to God. John states it afresh in another passage: 'No man has ever gone up into heaven; but there is one who has come down from heaven, the Son of Man who dwells in heaven.'[4] The three movements here are clearly marked. Christ is the Son of God who is in heaven; it is He who has come down from heaven; and that is why He alone has ascended into heaven. It is worth noticing that before the Gospel according to St. John, the Epistle to the Ephesians used almost the same expressions: 'The words, He has gone up, must mean that he had gone down, first, to the lower regions of the earth, And he who so went down is no other than he who has gone up, high above all the heavens.'[5] Thus alone can He who descended rise again. God alone can give man access to God.

This places the mystery of Christ in its own unique order. Nothing here bears any resemblance to those descending series of aeons which we find in the Gnostics; nothing implies that complicity with misery of which Nietzsche

[1] Cf. Simone Weil: 'Notice that in the Gospels there is never, unless I am mistaken, question of a search for God by man. In all the parables it is Christ who seeks men' (*Intimations of Christianity*, p. 1).—Trans.
[2] St. John 14 [6].   [3] St. John 1 [18].   [4] St. John 3 [13].   [5] Eph. 4 [9-10].

46

accused charity; nothing justifies humanization of the divine, in the sense of the reduction of transcendence. But Christ appears as the sovereign act of a transcendent God who, without repudiating any of His transcendence, comes to seek for that which is lost, not to transform Himself into it, but to transform it into Himself and raise it to His own sphere. For St. John, the transcendence of God is the sovereign freedom of a living God who is not bounded by anything, and whom it pleases to show forth His glory by performing wonderful works which disconcert human reason and have no other source than the free gift of His love.

And so in St. John's Gospel, Christ first of all bears witness to His belonging to the world of transcendence. It follows that He possesses, in all its fullness and by right of nature, the divine bounty in perfect equality with the Father, so that He can bestow it in a sovereign manner. This is true first of knowledge: 'None knows what the Father is, except the Son, and those to whom it is the Son's good pleasure to reveal him.'[1] Only the Son knows God as God knows Himself: 'Just as I am known to the Father, so I know him.'[2] The divine nature is a boundless ocean, a bottomless abyss. In its presence, man is seized with that giddiness which Gregory of Nyssa describes.[3] He has no longer anything to hold on to, he is totally deprived. Even when he is led by God's grace to grasp God as He is in Himself, such knowledge can never be complete. It will always remain in that luminous darkness whose boundaries He will never reach. Moreover, the knowledge of the Son is co-extensive with that infinite abyss, because it is knowledge of God by Himself. It is a total and exhaustive knowledge, for it is the expression of a perfect equality.

[1] St. Luke 10 [22].   [2] St. John 10 [15].
[3] See Jean Daniélou, *Platonisme et Théologie Mystique*, p. 130.

This is why Christ can bear witness to God. Already in St. Matthew's Gospel Christ declared: 'None knows the Father truly except the Son, and those to whom it is the Son's good pleasure to reveal him.'[1]   Christ is the only witness to God, in the sense that a witness is he who has seen: 'He bears witness of things he has seen and heard.'[2] For St. John, testimony is a fundamental category. There are two forms of testimony, that of the Son to the Father, and that of the Apostles to Christ. Thus everything depends upon the testimony of Christ. Faith consists in an absolute belief in that testimony, because it is not the testimony of someone from without, it is the testimony of someone exceedingly familiar with those things to which he is witnessing. In Christ, God bears witness to God, for God alone can bear witness to Himself. Thus we are brought into the realm of theology, which is the knowledge of God based upon the testimony of God. He is at once the way and the end. 'In Thy light we shall see light.'[3]

Just as the Son possesses the knowledge of the Father and can communicate that knowledge, so He possesses the life of the Father and can communicate this. 'As the Father has within him the gift of life, so he has granted to the Son that he too should have within him the gift of life.'[4] 'Life' means here the life of God, which is the Spirit. In this sense St. John writes elsewhere: 'In him there was life.'[5] In the New Testament life and death are theological conceptions. Life is the life of God and the sharing of that life, not biological existence. For the Bible, a man may be physically alive and spiritually dead, whilst on the other hand there is no one more alive than those among us

---

[1] St. Matt. 11 [27].   [2] St. John 3 [32]. See also 6 [46].
[3] Ps. 35 [10] (Vulgate), 36 [9] (Hebrew). Not the Knox version in this instance.
[4] St. John 5 [26].   [5] St. John 1 [4].

whom we call the dead, but who are alive in the life of God—the Virgin and the Saints. If Christ is not God, He does not possess this life and cannot communicate it. Thus it is upon the Divinity of Christ that faith in the Resurrection ultimately rests.

It is here that we realize to what an extent the Divinity of Christ, as St. John presents it, concerns the mystery of man at its very core. For man is the prisoner of death. He may seek to enlarge that prison through the progress of science, but he cannot escape from it. For his life remains always a corruptible life. So he comes up against the walls of his prison. 'His spirit raging against the cage,' said Claudel of Rimbaud. The prince of this world withholds the keys of the prison, and no man has power to take them from him. The Christian faith is that death, at once spiritual and bodily, the living death which is life apart from God, is vanquished by Christ in His Resurrection. But it is only if Christ is the Son of God that, descending into the prison of death, He has power to break the doors of the prison. This is only by virtue of the fact that He is the life which, joined with the corpse of man—a corpse which is His own— is able to kindle new life in it, and through His risen body to communicate this new life to our mortal body.

Thus, through the words of Christ in St. John's Gospel, there is disclosed the intimate bond between what Christ is and what Christ does. His task is to communicate the knowledge of the Father, to vivify with the life of the Father, to raise up man in order to bear him to the Father's bosom. This is what at the time He reveals and practises. Through this He manifests God's eternal design and the true meaning of human destiny, so that it is true, as Pascal said, that not only do we know God only through Jesus Christ, but we only know ourselves through Jesus Christ. But He only reveals and accomplishes this task in so far as He is the Son of God. If Christ is not God, we are still under the law of death, we are for ever locked in our prison, and night falls finally upon the world.

Everything turns upon the Divinity of Jesus. It is through this paradoxical claim that men see themselves. And this is just what John shows us. God sent His Son to save and not to condemn. But men can reject the life which the Son bears. And the Judgement is the act by which man judges himself: 'For the man who believes in Him, there is no rejection; the man who does not believe is already rejected; he has not found faith in the name of God's only-begotten Son. Rejection lies in this, that when the light came into the world men preferred darkness to light; preferred it, because their doings were evil.'[1] Thus in St. John's Gospel the conflict which the Synoptic Gospels show us with regard to the opposition of the Pharisees to Christ assumes more general proportions. Indeed it is no longer a question of the Pharisees. It is every man henceforth who is challenged not by Christ according to the flesh, but by Christ according to the Spirit. That is why unbelief is a sin against the Spirit, a refusal to leave the order of the flesh, a preference for darkness rather than the light.

This does not mean that recognition of the Divinity of Christ and belief in His Resurrection are things that come of their own accord. For we are creatures of flesh and blood, profoundly involved in animal life, adapted to the course of nature. It is an astounding adventure for creatures of flesh and blood to be plunged, in the midst of existence, into the abyss of the life of the Trinity, to see the Son of

[1] St. John 3 [18-19].

God taking human form and being called man, to become the Sons of God. This is absolutely unprecedented. It is understandable that unbelievers should find it difficult to accept. What is astonishing is that we are not more astonished ourselves, that our lives are not more radically transformed.

And yet this disconcerting claim which shatters our accustomed thoughts and upsets our pattern of behaviour, presents us in Christ with such a cumulative challenge that it is impossible to avoid facing the issue. Can the impossible have become the real? Is love the ultimate truth? What really resists in ourselves is the fear of the flesh before the invasion of a life which makes it divine; it is the confusion of a mind that is no longer sovereign master of its object. But by what right does reason or desire transport us to the frontiers of Love? What sort of complicity with death forces us to the conclusion that the truth is identified with the worst that can happen? There are certainly evil things to be reckoned with here, of which St. John speaks— things that lead to death. Men prefer the darkness, which is unhappiness, because they find it in themselves; and they reject the light, which is happiness, because they are compelled to acknowledge it as a gift.

So St. John clarifies the ultimate meaning of the fact presented by the Synoptics. From the outset it seems that the behaviour of Christ cannot be reduced to a purely rational explanation. It constitutes a riddle, a threshold before which mankind pauses, undecided. It marks a break with ordinary life. At first we assume that it follows the pattern of what is familiar to us, and we criticize it for departing from the patterns in which we see the laws of reality. We are like the people in Plato's cave, who are so accustomed to their darkness that they are hurt by the light.

So, like moles, we picture the universe in terms of the burrows in which we hide. But to those who receive Him, Christ is able to give the power to become the Sons of God; in other words, He makes them recognize that what they used to call their wisdom was only the wisdom of the flesh, and that He opens the eyes of the Spirit in those who know Him to be the real Wisdom.

Finally there remain the texts in which Christ allows us to glimpse something of His mysterious unity with the Father. Here it seems that the veil is rent, that the depth of life is revealed as an abyss of light. And this is indeed the impression which St. John's Gospel gives. The manhood of Christ becomes transparent, revealing the mysterious Trinity. The faith that first viewed Christ from the outside as a witness becomes the contemplation that penetrates directly to the object of His testimony. And there is in that contemplation a silent fullness which constitutes evidence in itself, which is unlike anything else, and in which the other side of things becomes in some way directly perceptible.

Similarly the saying: 'Thou Father, art in me, and I in thee,'[1] expresses the total reciprocal presence of the Father and the Son. This reciprocal presence is not something which is added to the Father and the Son as they are each first constituted in their own substance. But it is that very reciprocity in which they subsist, since it is only by their relationship that they are distinguished from one another. The Father is only the Father in so far as He eternally begets the Son. The Son is only the Son in so far as He is eternally begotten by the Father. And thus unchangeable eternity reveals in all its depth, inaccessible to man, beyond the veil, in the holy of holies, the eternal life of Love. And

[1] St. John 17 21.

this is no doubt the essential paradox to which we are accordingly granted access—the Three who are as primordial as the One, that is to say, Love inherent in the structure of absolute Being.

At this stage the movement is reversed. The sovereign Trinity now appears as the origin of all reality, and is no longer the objective towards which the ascent of man is laboriously directed. John first places us in the Trinity, and in Its light all else is explained and developed. Thus we may approach the Testimony of Christ from two sides. There is the testimony that arises from the immediately accessible fact of His manhood in His earthly life, a fact which gradually reveals through that manhood certain signs which lead us to recognize that it bears witness to another reality. And there is the testimony that places us instantly in that other reality, which is the testimony of the Son to the Father, offered in all its fiery splendour without any intervening stages. This second testimony is perhaps still more decisive. If the testimony of the mystics, that is, of those who have glimpsed a faint ray in the divine darkness, clearly conveys such impressive evidence, how much more that of the only Son, whose countenance radiates the glory of the Father, and who contains within Himself the fullness of Divinity!

It is this testimony that is revealed in the supreme words which are those of the high-priestly prayer. Here Christ declares Himself in all the dimensions of His eternal existence and His temporal mission as He who bestows sovereignly and eternally the life of the Father, since He is one with the Father—as He, moreover, who by virtue of that sovereign possession bestows eternal life upon those whom the Father has given Him. With Him eternity enters time, not to reduce itself to the level of time, but to raise time to the level of eternity. The ultimate ends of God's design are revealed. The Church appears as the introduction of humanity into the life of the Trinity, illuminated by the divine glory and gathered into the unity of Love.

There are no words like these: 'That they may all be one; that they, too, may be one in us, as thou Father art in me, and I in thee; so that the world may come to believe that it is thou who has sent me. And I have given them the privilege which thou gavest to me, that they should all be one, even as we are one; that while thou art in me, I may be in them, and so they may be perfectly made one.'[1] Christ appears here at once in His eternal being, and He is with the Church in His mission in time. He comes from the Father without ceasing to be close to Him, to seek the Church and bring her into the Father's presence. It is here the Divinity of Christ that reveals His Humanity. The latter draws its meaning from the relationship with God's design. It is the means by which the eternal Love which is in God is shown forth in the Church in order that she may be with God. If the Humanity of Christ led us to His Divinity, here it is His Divinity that makes clear the meaning of His Incarnation.

. . . . .

There remains one further source to record, that of the testimony borne to Jesus by the primitive Christian community. This is the testimony which raises fewest difficulties; indeed it is absolutely straightforward. The danger would be to consider no other evidence at all. This is what is done by certain representative of 'Form Criticism' like Dibelius or Bultmann. Considering quite justifiably that the New Testament is the testimony of faith of the early Christian community, they conclude that this

---

[1] St. John 17 21-23.

54

community certainly acknowledged Christ as the Son of God and the Lord. But they add that the Gospels enable us to grasp what the early Christians thought of Jesus, not what Jesus was or what He thought of Himself.

We may retain what is positive in this attitude and search for what the New Testament has to teach us of the faith of the community. And this is not without its importance. It is what we intend to do in this final section. But at the same time the negative aspect of the thesis we have mentioned is scientifically inadmissible. In fact the historical character of the life of Jesus seems unquestionable, as we have said in our first chapter. But Jesus' claim to Divinity forms part of this unquestionable historical pattern, for without it the drama of His life, which *is* the whole pattern, cannot be explained. If, then, the Gospels present Jesus through the faith of the primitive Church, they nevertheless present Jesus as He was in His historical reality. The testimony of the faith of the primitive Church therefore completes the testimony that Jesus gives of Himself; but it is by no means a substitute for it, and only makes sense by reference to it.

We shall bring forward the most important evidence that comes from the faith of the primitive Church, which is that of St. Paul. Here we are confronted by the earliest passages in the New Testament, which are also those with the most definite dates. Moreover, they come to us from a man who first saw Jesus as the leader of a heterodox sect, and who had been its persecutor. This man is a Jew in the strictest sense of the word, 'so fierce a champion was I of the traditions handed down by my forefathers.'[1] Consequently the mere idea of the deification of a creature must have been more intolerable to him than to anyone

[1] Gal. i 14.

else. If, therefore, he has testified that Jesus of Nazareth was the Son of God, it was because he was driven to it by evidence that ran counter to his whole psychological bent. Accordingly he is in this sense an exceptional witness.

Moreover, his evidence is decisive. For Paul, Jesus of Nazareth is God Himself who has come into this world. He expresses this in some degree by three concentric statements that rise from the work of Christ to His Person. And that is undoubtedly the characteristic feature of St. Paul's testimony. In this it differs from the witnesses to Christ's earthly life. For Paul, Christ is primarily the risen Christ in whom the redemptive work of God is revealed. But in other respects he maintains the strict continuity of the risen Christ, who appeared to him on the road to Damascus, with Jesus of Nazareth whose disciples he was persecuting. The words of Christ addressed to him express this fundamental statement: 'I am Jesus whom Saul persecutes.'[1]

Paul's first testimony is that in Jesus a strictly divine act is accomplished. In this respect he puts himself in line with the Jewish faith, which is faith in a God who intervenes in human history. But Paul's claim, exactly put, is that in Jesus there takes place a divine act which is the decisive act of God, constituting the salvation of the world. This divine act is described by St. Paul in a series of expressions that reveal its various aspects. First of all there is justification: 'But, in these days, God's way of justification has at last been brought to light; one which was attested by the law and the prophets, but stands apart from the law; God's way of justification through faith in Jesus Christ, meant for everybody and sent down upon everybody without distinction, if he has faith. . . . And justification

[1] Acts 9 [5].

comes to us as a free gift from his grace, through our redemption in Christ Jesus.'[1]

This is a key passage because it places us at the very source of the Pauline declaration. It shows that its roots are in Judaism. Righteousness (*tsedeq*) is a key idea in the Old Testament, expressing a strictly divine mode of action through which God irrevocably achieves the fulfilment of His promises. The object of this divine action is to establish man in righteousness, that is, in a state of holiness which makes him pleasing to God. But this very question of justification occupied a key position in Jewish theology in the time of St. Paul. By contrast with the Pharisees of his period, the Teacher of Righteousness was already maintaining that man is by himself fundamentally corrupted, and that God alone can establish him in a state of righteousness.[2] But in calling upon this righteousness he was groaning beneath the weight of his sin. The Fourth Book of Esdras also shows us mankind beneath the sin of the fact of Adam's fall, and the impossibility of righteousness for man.

It is in this perspective that we find St. Paul's saying: 'All alike have sinned, all alike are unworthy of God's praise.'[3] The whole of mankind is therefore deprived of righteousness and unable to obtain it, being entirely under sin. What is accomplished in Jesus is precisely an action of God bestowing righteousness, an absolutely free and gratuitous act, a strictly divine decision, which removes man from the desperate situation in which he was living. This act is carried out in Jesus Christ, and the condition for benefiting from it is therefore to believe in Jesus Christ and in the object of that testimony, which is also

---

[1] Rom. 3 21-24.
[2] See Jean Daniélou, *Les manuscrits de la Mer Morte et les origines du christianisme*, pp. 95–96.   [3] Rom. 3 23.

Jesus Christ, in so far as He is Himself that divine act which works righteousness through His Incarnation, Passion and Resurrection: 'God ... has vindicated the holiness of Jesus Christ, here and now, as one who is himself holy, and imparts holiness to those who take their stand upon faith in him.'[1]

This justifying action of God is described in terms that bring to light its various aspects. It is redemption (λύτρωσις). This word is already used in the Old Testament to convey the action of God in so far as He frees man from a desperate position. It means particularly the way in which God, by His power alone, delivered the captive people from Egypt by dividing the waters of the Red Sea before them:[2] 'They are thy people, thy dear possession, rescued by thee so signally, with such display of thy power!'[3] It is therefore a kindred work that is performed in Jesus Christ, but at a far more essential level. It implies that mankind is in a state of captivity: 'You were the slaves of sin.'[4] No human power could deliver us from this captivity. But God by His mighty power brought about our liberation. Jesus Christ is the act of deliverance. And it is accomplished in the blood of His Cross, making it clear that the manhood of Christ is the instrument by which the divine act is effected.

This divine act is also the central communication of righteousness, that is to say of holiness: 'Now you have been sanctified, now you have been justified in the name of the Lord Jesus, by the Spirit of the God we serve.'[5] 'Holiness' is in the Old Testament, and particularly from the time of Isaiah onward, is the term used to define the life of God in respect of that which distinguishes absolutely between the life of the Creator and the life of the creature. God is

[1] Rom. 3 [26].   [2] Exod. 14.   [3] Deut. 9 [29].   [4] Rom. 6 [17].   [5] I Cor. 6 [11].

58

the Holy One. To sanctify, therefore, means to communicate the life of God, that which He alone can do, that which is supremely the divine activity. And this sanctification is precisely salvation, for the latter consists in removing man from the spiritual death, which is sin, and communicating to him spiritual life, which is the very life of God. Sanctification is thus the gift of the life of the Spirit, which makes of man a spiritual being. And that is strictly the work which God's power alone accomplishes.

Sanctification betokens the divine act that gives life to souls. But this life-giving act accomplished in Christ also affects man in his body, which is dead in that it is mortal— in other words, in that it is bound to the misery of its biological condition. In Christ, the action of God penetrates this mortal body with divine energy and bestows upon it an incorruptible form of life. God's action first brought this process into operation in the mortal humanity of Christ Himself. That is why the Resurrection of Christ is for St. Paul the point on which the whole faith rests: 'If Christ has not risen, all your faith is a delusion; you are back in your sins.'[1] Here we can see clearly how the testimony of St. Paul bears primarily upon the divine acts accomplished in Christ. This raising, which first applied to the manhood of Christ, is also to apply eschatologically to every man who has believed. Thus God's righteousness is to complete to the full its divinizing task.

In this first series of testimonies, St. Paul declares that in Jesus Christ the decisive divine act intervened, that it constitutes the essential happening of sacred history. In this his theology is in line with the Old Testament, which bore witness to divine acts and heralded an eschatological action of God which was to be the decisive action. On

---

[1] 1 Cor. 15 [17].

another level Paul shows how this divine action is not only God's action, but that it involves sharing in the life of the Son of God, and therefore that it is in so far as He is the Son of God that Christ brings about in us the sharing of His life. In other words, it is not only a question of communicating the divine life, but of communicating the life of the Son of God. Consequently it is in being made one with the Son of God that men fulfil God's plan. This is the Pauline doctrine of adoption, in which the personal role of the Son of God takes precedence over the action of God viewed in a general way.

A key passage shows the connexion between this theme and that of righteousness: 'All those who from the first were known to Him, he has destined from the first to be moulded into the image of his Son, who is thus to become the eldest born among many brethren. So predestined, he called them; so called, he justified them; so justified, he glorified them.'[1] Here the stages of the divine acts worked in Christ are displayed: calling, justification, glorification, are the successive moments in an eternal design whose end is adoption, since its object is to mould the Christian in the image of the Son, in other words to bestow upon him by a free and unprecedented gift the divine privileges which the Son possesses by His nature. The doctrine of adoption adds this Trinitarian aspect which is characteristic of the New Testament, and in which the Person of the incarnate Word is established at the centre of God's design.

This doctrine is further developed in the Epistle to the Ephesians where the term 'adoption' explicitly appears, and where the function of individual humanity assumed by the Son of God takes on its central character: 'He has chosen us out, in Christ, before the foundation of the world, to be

[1] Rom. 8 29-30.

saints, to be blameless in his sight, for love of him; marking us out beforehand (so his will decreed) to be his adopted children through Jesus Christ. Thus he would manifest the splendour of that grace by which he has taken us into his favour in the person of his beloved Son.'[1] Thus the centre of God's design becomes the very Person of Christ the Son of God. It is in him first of all that the work of God is accomplished which joins divine nature to human nature. It is in him 'and through his blood, that we have redemption, the forgiveness of our sins.'[2] God's design is thus to enable us to share through faith in what has first been fulfilled in His Person.

This sharing in the life of the Son is bestowed by the gift of the Spirit, who alone can accomplish the divine work of adoption, being God Himself: 'The appointed time came. Then God sent out his Son on a mission to us. He took birth from a woman, took birth as a subject of the law, so as to ransom those who were subject to the law, and make us sons by adoption. To prove that you are sons, God has sent out the Spirit of his Son into your hearts, crying out in us, Abba, Father.'[3] The gift of the Spirit not only grants incorruptibility, it causes man strictly to share in the life of the Son. It introduces him into the sphere of the Trinity. Henceforth, man is no longer simply on the level of bondage, which is that of the creature; he can be with God as with a Father, in so far as he is joined with the only Son: 'The Spirit you have now received is not, as of old, a spirit of slavery, to govern you by fear; it is the spirit of adoption, which makes us cry out, Abba, Father.'[4]

Finally, in a third stage, St. Paul enlarges his perspective. He not only shows the role of the Person of the Son in

[1] Eph. 1 [4-6].   [2] Eph. 1 [7].   [3] Gal. 4 [4-6].   [4] Rom. 8 [15].

the mystery of adoption, but he shows His mystery as constituting the very centre of the divine plan. This appears first in a key passage in the Epistle to the Philippians in which Paul shows us Jesus Christ, existing in the form (ἐν μορφῇ) of God, possessing equality with God, and dispossessing (ἐκένωσεν) Himself and taking upon Himself in this state of dispossession the nature of man, but exalted afterwards by God who has given to Him the name which is above every other name.[1] Thus Christ appears, as we have already seen in St. John, in successive stages of His mystery: first as pre-existing in His divine state and possessing the divine nature in all its fullness; then as seeking for human nature in its fallen state and taking the form of a servant; and finally as glorified in that same nature which, through the Ascension, is exalted above every creature into the very sphere of transcendent Divinity.

The manhood of Christ becomes the centre of Paul's vision. It is this that is viewed in its successive stages. And it is in this that God's plan is first accomplished. Indeed, it is chiefly through Christ's manhood that the end of creation, the glory of God, is attained. Accepting 'an obedience which brought him to death,' Christ, through His human will, renders perfect glory to God and is thus made the high priest of the whole creation. It is the priestly character of the Person of Christ that the Epistle to the Hebrews is to develop, by showing Christ as the high priest after the order of Melchisedech. On the other hand, it is in and through the manhood of Christ that the other purpose of creation is achieved, namely the divinization of man, since the Father gives Christ 'that name which is greater than any other name' by raising His manhood to

[1] Cf. Phil. 2 ⁵⁻⁹.

the level of divine glory, whence it radiates that glory upon the rest of mankind.

In the Epistle to the Colossians, Paul gives this role of Christ cosmic dimensions. He shows Him as first exercising His mission in the creation of the world: 'He is the true likeness of the God we cannot see; his is that first birth which precedes every act of creation. Yes, in him all created things took their being, heavenly and earthly, visible and invisible; what are thrones and dominions, what are princedoms and powers? They were all created through him and in him; and he takes precedency of all, and in him all things subsist.'[1] Here Paul is at one with the Prologue to St. John's Gospel: 'All things came into being through Him.' He illuminates the mystery of Christ by giving Him a title which the Old Testament gave to the Wisdom of God, which is 'his image.'[2] The Epistle to the Hebrews uses similar phrases: 'He is the radiance of his Father's Splendour and the full expression of his being;[3] all creation depends, for its support, on his enabling word.'[4] We may say that the claims of the New Testament here achieve their most dazzling epitome, asserting in fact that He who dies on the Cross is He who upholds all things in their being. The Fathers of the Church were to develop this contrast in their *Paschal Homilies*. We read in that of Melito of Sardis in the second century: 'He who hung the Earth is hanged (on the tree). He who fixed the heavens is fixed (to the cross). He who secured the heavens is secured on the tree.'[5] Christ appears as the pre-existing Son of God, but He appears also as having a special relationship with creation. It is by Him that all things were made, and the creation thus belongs to Him by special right. Sacred

[1] Col. 1 15-17.   [2] Wisd. 7 26.   [3] Wisd. 2 24.   [4] Heb. 1 3.   [5] 96, Lohse, p. 34.

history thus enlarges the dimensions of cosmic history. It embraces not only mankind, but Dominions and Powers. And by the same token the coming of Christ takes on a cosmic perspective. It no longer concerns mankind alone, but also Principalities and Powers.

This is what the sequel to Paul's text shows. It is the same Son of God who created the world and to whom the world belongs, who returns to take possession of it in the Incarnation, and who establishes it in its final state, thus fulfilling God's design: 'He too is that head whose body is the Church; it begins with him since his was the first birth out of death; thus in every way the primacy was to become his. It was God's good pleasure to let all completeness dwell in him, and through him to win back all things, whether on earth or in heaven, into union with himself, making peace with them through his blood, shed on the cross.'[1] Thus the action of Christ in His Passion reaches out to the entire universe, reconciling it to God, and at the same time restoring its unity. And thus the glorified Manhood of Christ becomes the summit and centre of that universe, the crown of God's creation. All is not only 'by Him' but 'for Him.'

. . . . .

This investigation of the New Testament provides us with three facts that cannot be seriously disputed. Jesus of Nazareth, a person whose historical existence is as securely established as that of Socrates or Caesar, showed by His whole attitude that He claimed strictly divine authority and powers, stated explicitly that He belonged to an order of reality other than that of this world, and that He shared in the nature and attributes of the Father in all its fullness, was recognized as the Son of God, and as God Himself

[1] Col. I 18-20.

by men who were His contemporaries and in every way predisposed to regard such a claim as the most unacceptable of blasphemies.

This does not remove from Christ's claims anything of their absolutely unprecedented and humanly impossible character. The only reaction of a clear intellect is bound to be, at first, to reject these claims, and to do so in proportion as it fails to recognize their right to acceptance. Nothing would be more contrary to the very nature of Christ's claim than to treat it as something which happened of its own accord. Nevertheless it must be admitted that the claim is put forward with a unity and continuity which make it impossible to dispose of it. For two thousand years it has challenged every man with a decisive question, *the* decisive question. It is ultimately impossible, if one investigates it seriously, not to admit that it constitutes a unique fact of nature, irreducible to any rational explanation, and that it is reasonable to accept it in spite of its improbable character. Christ's claim is not made, however, without a full background; and it is this background which we have now to consider.

BIBLIOGRAPHY

L. DE GRANDMAISON, *La personne de Jésus et ses témoins*, Paris, 1957.

K. L. SCHMIDT, *Le problème du christianisme primitif*, Paris, 1938.

O. CULLMANN, *Christ and Time*, London, 1951. *La Christologie du Nouveau Testament*, Paris, 1958.

L. CERFAUX, *Christ in the Theology of Saint Paul*, London, 1960.

J. DUPONT, *Essai sur la christologie de saint Jean*, Bruges, 1951.

CHAPTER III

PROPHECIES AND TYPES

CHRIST, at the level where He is part of a historical situation through being what He was, constitutes an irreducible 'datum,' an order apart. But this cries out to be interpreted, and it rests upon us to discover what we should relate him to. Now Christ Himself—and the New Testament writers after Him—has done precisely this. Christ places Himself in the continuity of the Old Testament scheme of things. For it was by relating Himself to the latter that He never ceased to explain Himself. As Wilhelm Visher has said, 'The New Testament tells us who Christ is. The Old Testament tells us what Christ is.' Christ is not a disconnected entity, as Marcion made out, but something quite intelligible. This intelligibility, however, is not the result of rational analysis or of tracing a historical source. It is an intelligibility which is found within the framework of the Bible, putting us in touch with an order of reality that has its own proper laws, the order of sacred history, the order of the mighty works of God.

This order of reality is not to be approached by rational demonstration. It springs, indeed, from God's interventions, which surpass the demands of reason. 'Such things are made of love,' as Guardini writes. But these divine interventions display such exact analogies amongst themselves, present such a remarkable unity, that they provide a formidable array of evidence. In this sense we may say that the details of sacred history are proved by the whole corpus of sacred history. In other respects they are so disconcerting to human logic that they cannot possibly be the product of it, but introduce us to an order which surpasses it and whose reasons are not those of Reason. These, then, are the biblical categories that provide the unfolding of the New Testament with its formularies. Therefore it is not a question, as Bultmann thought, of mythical categories that represent only a symbolic expression of a reality which in itself is inaccessible, but of the ways of God which have already been revealed in the Old Testament and which find their fulfilment in the New Testament.

This relationship of Christ with the Old Testament must first be justified. We must show what it is that forms its basis, and ensures that it is not in any way arbitrary. For this purpose we must first of all show what is involved in the claims which the Old Testament puts forward. Only when these are established can we be sure of a solid basis for the 'Demonstration of the Gospel' (to make use of an expression of Eusebius of Caesarea). It is with the Old Testament that there appears the order of reality to which Christ is to belong. In this sense the choosing of Abraham, which inaugurates the story of God's people, marks a definite threshold and involves already the basic truths of which Christ is to be the supreme expression.

What are these truths? The first and the one which brooks no denial is that of the existence of the *magnalia Dei*, that is, of divine interventions into the pattern of human history. It is not necessary to be a Judaeo-Christian in order to believe in the existence of a god.[1] This is to be found in all religions, and is the mark of religion as such. But it is necessary to be a Judaeo-Christian to believe in the intervention of God in human history. To return to a distinction we have already made, religion is the expression of man's quest for God; it is the movement of man towards

[1] The original has 'd'un Dieu.'

God. Revelation is the expression of God's quest for man;
it is the movement of God towards man. Apart from this,
the whole of Christianity disappears. Apart from it, indeed,
Christianity is no longer anything but one religion among
others, even if it is, absolutely speaking, the highest of
them. Now this truth is already presented by the Old
Testament. And in a sense the Old Testament is already
the Incarnation before the Incarnation.

This first glance at the topic already brings into relief
a number of essential elements to which we shall have
occasion to refer in speaking of Christ. There is first of all
the question of facts, contingent events, with all the
apparent arbitrariness that this implies. Why was it
Abraham who was chosen, and not someone else? This
occurrence must be given its unique significance, and it
must not be turned into a symbol. Any reduction of the
events of the Old and New Testaments to mythical schemes
causes their essential meaning to disappear. The real
difference between myth and mystery is that the former
expresses a projection of the permanent needs of the
human soul, whilst the latter is a fact, concrete and
absolutely unique. Simone Weil's mistake was to try to
assimilate the gallows on which Christ hung to the cosmic
pillar of Indian mythology. In this way she reduced the
Christian event to unqualified religiosity.

On the other hand we are concerned with divine facts.
For the reason, this constitutes a paradox. Certainly these
acts consist in changes that affect men. But they are changes
brought about solely by the power of God. These strictly
divine acts are precisely those which the Old Testament
describes for us, and which we find again in the New
Testament. They constitute, as it were, the grammar of
faith. Creation is one of them, and consists in bringing

it about that something should *be* where formerly there was nothing; and it is the expression of the sovereign power of the Divine. Covenant is another divine act, which consists, on God's side, in raising man above his created condition to enable him to share permanently in the benefits that are proper to him. Deliverance is the third, releasing man from a desperate situation by an act of God's sole power. And so also it is with Abiding, Judgement, Adoption, Election.

These divine acts comprise sacred history, rightly understood—the context of the coming of Christ. There is also profane history, that of civilization, which tells of the mighty works of man, and sings the praises of his genius. But there is sacred history, too, the history of salvation, which tells of the mighty works of God and sings of the glory of God. It is to this sacred history that Christ belongs. 'He did not make great discoveries,' said Pascal, 'but he was holy, holy, holy, to God, striking terror into the Devil.' So He springs from an order of greatness which is strictly that of holiness. For the order of wisdom, to which Buddha and Socrates belong, is related only to the order of human greatness. Christ is not primarily a great religious personality, He is primarily an act of God among men. And that is why it is a perfectly accurate method of conducting one's reasoning to judge of Christ, not in the spirit of geometry or subtlety, which relate to the order of bodies and minds, but in the spirit of prophecy, which concerns the order of holiness.

Finally, these acts of God have as their object the uplifting of man. If he who accomplishes them is God, he in whom and for whom they are accomplished is man. In this sense whatever happens is a happening which concerns man and not a happening which concerns God. And this happening has a content which is wholly positive.

The world of bodies and minds is not, in the viewpoint of the Bible, a kind of 'debasement' of the divine Unity. The creative act establishes the world for what it really is, a divine outgrowth. On the level of the spirit, it establishes it in all its free and conscious being—the expression of creative Love, which is essentially the communication of being, and whose tendency is to give rise to life and to lead onward to their fulfilment the works which it has begotten. This remains true of the other works of God. In the Covenant, it calls upon those whom it has created to share in the life which is its own. Thus the Covenant is the characteristic act of faithful love, by which God raises the creature about Himself and thus reveals His hidden plan. The Covenant is the expression of all that God seeks to fulfil in man, revealing what man is, having first shown us what God is. Deliverance in its turn indicates God's work in man in the context of sin. Thus the works of God are concerned with man's divine calling.

The second characteristic of the Old Testament is prophecy. Indeed, if we read the Old Testament, we come to the conclusion that its object is not only to bear witness to the great works which God has performed in the world and in history in past times, but to herald those which He will perform in the future. This is strictly the message of the Prophets, and in a certain sense it is the most important. The Old Testament only tells us what God has done in the past in order to establish an expectation of what He will do in the future. The basis of this expectation is God's faithfulness to His promises.

We shall understand the whole import of such a statement if we compare it once more with the attitude of other religions. The natural inclination of the pagan soul is towards nostalgia for the past. We have explained this in a previous volume.[1] For the pagan, reality is that which exists in the era of myth before real time begins. For him, time can never do anything except to degrade what existed primordially in a perfect manner. The aim of his ritual, therefore, is to preserve contact with that mythical past. Paradise is inevitably Paradise Lost. This is the natural inclination of the human soul when left to itself, an inclination which expresses itself in the sort of poetry that consists of nostalgia for the lost Paradise of childhood impressions. In Proust or Rilke it appears in fragments from childhood mysteriously withdrawn from the destructive action of time. And that is why it despairs of entering again into Paradise alive.

Now in direct opposition to this point of view stands the paradoxical assertion of prophecy, which bases its claim not on human probability but on divine veracity alone, and proclaims that the essential event has yet to take place. It thus gives meaning and stability to the temporal order and lays the foundations of a historical vision of man and the universe by conferring value and intelligibility upon history. It culminates in a new wisdom, which does not consist, like that of the Platonists and the Hindus, in escaping from evil time, nor, like the Stoics and Buddhists, in renouncing desire, but on the contrary in a calm expectation of what God is about to do—and this is called hope. And so, in relating Christ to prophecy, the New Testament places Him at the centre of a theology of history. This is the problem of Christ and Time, to the importance of which Oscar Cullmann has drawn attention.

Prophecy has several features that are relevant to what we shall have occasion to discuss below. It establishes a relationship between the past and future works of God.

[1] *God and Us*, 1956.

On the one hand there is a fundamental analogy between these works. The new creation will be a taking-up-again of the first creation, and the new Exodus will be a deliverance like the old. And this means quite simply that, being the work of the same God, they reveal the ways of God, which are the same. By this means the legitimacy of the comparison between past works and future works is established. This mutual relationship is called typology. It provides a permanent context, an order of things that presents reliable laws. It is within this context that the mystery of Christ is to be inscribed. Prophecy in the field of the historical conception of the Bible is analogous to a generalization in the field of the logical development of reason, a movement towards a limit which abstracts the fact from its contingent circumstances and confers upon it the value of a principle.

First of all, prophecy brings with it the paradoxical statement that the works which God will perform in the future are greater than those which He has performed in the past. This is Isaias' leitmotive: 'Do not remember those old things, as if you had eyes for nothing but what happened long ago; I mean to perform new wonders; even now they are coming to the birth.'[1] This text clearly refers to the Exodus. Now the crossing of the Red Sea was for the Jews the most significant memory in their history, the supreme work performed by God on their behalf. Nevertheless, what Isaias proclaims is greater still. The New Exodus is to obliterate the memory of the Old.

But prophecy is no mere forecast of the coming of an event that will form part of the ordinary pattern of history. It has essentially a bearing upon the end of history. It is of its very nature eschatological. Its purpose is to proclaim

[1] Isa. 43 18-19.

the end of time and the supreme acts that God will perform at the end of time. Accordingly we should not expect from it any precise circumstantial details. This would be a case of turning prophecy into a kind of empirical fore-knowledge of what does not yet exist, and not on a theological statement concerning the structure of God's plan. That empirical knowledge, 'that day and that hour' no one knows—'not the angels of heaven; only the Father knows them.'[1] The prophesies of Isaias have nothing in common with the predictions of Nostradamus. God is not seeking to satisfy our curiosity, but to lead us into His ways.

This is of the utmost consequence with regard to the application of prophecies to Christ. Christ fulfils prophecies in so far as He fulfils eschatology and is therefore the final event. It would be childish to suppose that Matthew's application of Osee's prophecy: 'I called my son out of Egypt'[2] to the flight of Jesus to Egypt and His return, had this detail of the life of Christ as its essential object. It suffices to re-read it in its full context to see that its object is the Fatherhood of God towards Israel, and that its meaning is to show us in Jesus the true Israel. Matthew added it to the episode of the flight to Egypt because of the reference to Egypt, but it could just as well have been added to some other episode.

In the same way, when John tells us, at the most solemn moment in his Gospel, with regard to the crucified Jesus: 'This was so ordained to fulfil what is written, You shall not break a single bone of His,'[3] it would clearly be absurd to see in the unbroken bones of the Paschal lamb a prophecy of the unbroken bones of Christ. John's purpose is to show us the Paschal lamb in the crucified Christ.

[1] St. Matt. 24 36.   [2] St. Matt. 2 15. Hos. 11 1.   [3] St. John 19 36.

73

Moreover, as is often the case in the Gospel, springing from the culture of the period, the verse which is quoted is not necessarily the most important one. It is merely an invitation to re-read the full text, whose equivalent would be the footnotes in our modern books! The most famous example is verse 1 of Psalm 21, which the Evangelists place in the mouth of Christ on the Cross, inviting us to apply the whole Psalm to Christ, in default of which we should commit a very serious misrepresentation by seeing a cry of despair where it is a question, on the contrary, of a prayer of trust.[1]

These references, however, need not be confined to words. They may refer to the actions of Christ, intended to show the relationship of a certain work of His to the prophecies of the Old Testament. Even then the essential thing is not the material detail, but the meaning it conveys. Thus the action of Jesus in asking His apostles to find an ass in preparation for His entry into Jerusalem doubtless implies that He wished to show by this that He was fulfilling the prophecy of Zacharias which describes for us the Messianic king.[2] In fact it is obvious that what Christ meant to show by this action was that He was the Messianic king and that consequently, as the Gospel well says, He did this 'to fulfil the word spoken by the prophet,'[3] in short, to emphasize that the prophecy was fulfilled in Him.

We must recall these ideas in order to explain the meaning of the references to Christ in the Old Testament. The proper object of the New Testament from this point of view is, therefore, to proclaim that in Christ the eschatological events, the 'Last Days' heralded by the Prophets, have come to pass. We read, for example, in the Epistle

---

[1] See Jean Daniélou, 'Le Psaume XXI dans le catéchisme patristique, *Maison Dieu*, 49 (1957), pp. 17–34. (Ps. 22 in Hebrew).
[2] Zach. ⁹.   [3] St. Matt. 21 ⁴.

to the Hebrews: 'In old days, God spoke to our fathers
in many ways and by many means, through the prophets;
now at last in these times he has spoken to us with a Son
to speak for him.'[1] Or again, He has been revealed once
for all, at the moment when history reached its fulfilment,
annulling our sin by His sacrifice.[2] All these expressions
denote the eschatological times proclaimed by the Prophets.
These times are henceforth 'to-day.' So the New Testament
is essentially the presence of the eschatological event. Its
purpose is not to teach us the existence of Paradise, nor to
promise us this Paradise in the future, but to show us this
Paradise already present in Christ: 'This day thou shalt
be with me in Paradise.'[3] It is not the proclamation of
Judgement to come, but of Judgement already here:
'Sentence is now being passed on this world; now is the
time when the prince of this world is to be cast out.'[4]
The Old Testament proclaimed that a servant of God
would be a lamb sacrificed for the sins of the world.[5] The
New Testament shows us 'the Lamb of God . . . he who
takes away the sin of the world.'[6] And it teaches us that
with the coming of this Lamb, the fate of mankind is at
once unveiled and dislosed, that the Last Things are
revealed and fulfilled.[7] Christ, as C. H. Dodd says, is
'realized eschatology.'

This again is an extraordinary assertion. It was already
a paradoxical statement, as against the pagan religions of
the past, to claim that the decisive event was to be expected
in the future. But now, by contrast with the modern
ideas of evolution, the Gospel claims that the key event
has already happened. No evolution, no invention, no
revolution, will ever produce anything as important as

---

[1] Heb. 1 [1-2].   [2] Heb. 9 [26].   [3] St. Luke 23 [43].
[4] Cp. St. John 12 [31].   [5] Cp. Isa. 53 [7].   [6] St. John 1 [29].
[7] Apoc. 5 [6-7].

the resurrection of Jesus Christ. This, in the phrase that reappears in the Epistle to the Hebrews, is accomplished for all, at the moment when history reached its fulfilment. It is not only the end of an order of things, but the end of all things. It challenges every futurist conception, every claim to surpass it. Jesus Christ cannot be surpassed, because there is nothing beyond Jesus Christ. And there is nothing beyond Jesus Christ because there cannot be anything beyond Him.

If this is so, it is in Jesus Christ that the work of God begun by creation finally reaches its goal. It is not only a question of an end in which something ceases that could have continued to exist. It is an end in the sense of a goal that is perfectly attained. Now in Christ the goal pursued by God reaches its fulfilment. In Him the two purposes of God's plan are truly accomplished in all their fullness. On the one hand, human nature is raised to a sharing in the good things of God, such as could not possibly be more intimate. In the Person of Christ, in fact, through the hypostatic union, man is united with God in a sharing of blessings such as could not possibly be more intimate, and that in an absolutely indissoluble manner. Thus there is accomplished substantially and for ever in Christ the uplifting of man, which is his divinization, in such a way as to enable all men to share in that which was first established in Him. This is the new and eternal Covenant which consummates the mystery of the Covenant.

On the other hand, in Christ, God is perfectly glorified. The glorification of God is also an end of creation. Now only Christ's Manhood united with the Word accomplishes this, when Christ makes Himself obedient to death and the death of the Cross. This constitutes the perfect priestly act. Christ, established as sovereign priest by the fact of the hypostatic union itself, offers in His Passion the new and eternal sacrifice which abolishes all other sacrifices and becomes the rightful expression of the worship rendered to God by the whole of creation. Thus creation achieves its end, which is to glorify God. It is indeed 'by Him, with Him and in Him' that all glory goes up to the Almighty Father. It is not only the history of Israel, nor that of mankind, but that of the entire creation which finds its completion in the Paschal mystery, a cosmic mystery which resounds to the limits of the world of bodies and spirits.

This does not mean that after the coming of Christ upon earth history does not still continue. But it does mean that history is not a 'going-beyond' of Christ, in the sense of outstripping Him. The risen Christ remains the content of history, which now consists only in the unfolding throughout the whole of mankind of what was first accomplished in Him. In this sense Christ, the end of history, is also the centre of history, in that everything that comes before Him prepared the way for Him, and everything that comes after Him issues from Him. The mystery of Christ in its entirety constitutes the end of history. But that end reveals itself in successive stages. One part is already fulfilled in the historic mysteries of Christ. Another is in course of fulfilment in the present life of the Church. Another, the glorious Parousia, is still awaited.

These principles govern the whole Christian view of things, but for the moment we are concerned with one particular aspect. Our intention was to establish the legitimacy of the application to Christ of the categories of the Old Testament to provide the context in which to place Him. It is this conclusion which remains to be drawn. We have said that prophecy showed us in eschatological

events the renewal of the mighty works of God in the Old
Testament. Now we have just seen that these eschatological
events were accomplished in Christ. Accordingly we have
the right to consider that the events of the life of Christ are
truly the renewal, in a more perfect and final manner, of
the mighty works of God in the Old Testament. Old and
New Testaments are successive states in the same divine
plan in which are revealed the same ways of God.

Thus types and prophecies (τύποι and λόγοι) fit one into
another and complete each other. Prophecy indeed provides
the justification of typology. Its object is not only to
proclaim eschatological events, it also shows that these
events will be the taking-up-again on a grander scale of the
actions of God in the past history of Israel. Thus the Gospel
demonstration is unfolded in three phases. The Law bears
witness to the mighty works of God in the world and in
His people. Prophecy proclaims that Yahweh is to perform
analogous works, but far greater ones. It therefore constitutes an eschatological typology, in which the *magnalia Dei*
of the people of Israel appear as types of the eschatological
magnalia Dei. Thus is typology already found in the Old
Testament.

The New Testament bears witness that the eschatological *magnalia Dei* are henceforth accomplished in Christ.
By the same token, the mighty works of the Old Testament,
of which they were the anti-type, become types of Christ
in whom eschatology is fulfilled. Thus the story of salvation
is displayed as the story of the mighty works of God
in the different phases of the fulfilment of His plan. And
we see established the context in which the Person and
work of Christ are placed. An examination of His attitude
and behaviour shows us that it is impossible to dissolve
away the fact of Christ into mere historical immanence.

As for those aspects of Christ which stand apart from human history, the Old Testament provides us with the means of 'placing' them. These aspects arise from a particular order, and the fact that they relate to that order gives them intelligibility. It now remains to be said that the Old Testament is not sufficient for the purpose of defining their character. We must therefore discover a fresh approach to it.

.   .   .   .   .

If we now return to the content of the Old Testament as Holy Scripture reveals it to us, we must admit that it contains diverse elements. On the one hand its purpose is to describe for us the *mirabilia*, the mighty works of God, and to proclaim the renewal of these mighty works in the future. And in this sense the content of Scripture is first of all the creation, both of the world and of man; it is the Covenant made with Moses and the giving of the Law which accompanies it; it is the miraculous deliverance from Egypt of the captive people and the protection that is granted to them in their Exodus to the Promised Land; it is the abiding presence of Yahweh in the Temple at Jerusalem and His kingship over the people whom He has raised up for Himself.

Consequently, what is expected at the end of time are divine acts similar to these, but far surpassing them in splendour. The Prophets, like the Apocalypse, proclaim that Yahweh shall create 'new heavens and a new earth,' having no need of the sun, for God Himself will be its light.[1] The Prophets announce that Yahweh will establish a new Covenant more marvellous than the first, and will give a Law which shall be written not on tables of stone, but in human hearts. They promise the persecuted people a

[1] Isa. 65 17. Rev. 21 1, 23.

deliverance which will be more wonderful than that of the Exodus from all their enemies, and one in which the power and love of God will reveal themselves in all their fullness. They describe the eschatological Temple in which Yahweh will dwell in the midst of a sanctified people, over whom His reign will be finally established.

Besides this approach, there is another which is to be clearly distinguished from it. The Old Testament shows us a number of persons who play a decisive part in sacred history and are its protagonists, chosen by God. Thus Abraham is the first to respond to God's call and appears as the first-born of the chosen people; Moses is, above all, the ambassador who leads the people out of Egypt, who communicates to it the Law of God; David is chosen to reign over the people of Israel and to be the shepherd who guides them; Elias is sent to the faithless people to remind them of the Covenant made on Sinai and to bring them back into the ways of righteousness; Isaias proclaims deliverance to the captive people and reveals to them the mystery of God most Holy.

Following the principle which requires that prophecy should be the proclamation for the future of the renewal of past events, the expectation of Israel will therefore be directed towards the eschatological coming of persons who will be in a more perfect degree what those of the past have already been. The Prophets herald a new Moses who shall be the true Prophet, the instrument of supreme revelations; they herald a new David, the Messianic king whose reign shall be without end; they herald a new Adam, who shall lead man back to the Paradise which was lost by the first Adam; they herald another Jonas, who shall be delivered not merely from a sea-monster, but from the Beast of the Sea which holds man in its power. These

persons are at once God's instruments in His acts on behalf
of His people, and also those in whom these divine acts
are carried out.

What the New Testament is to reveal, which the Old
Testament did not make clear, is that these two distinct
approaches meet in the Person of Jesus.[1] On the one hand
there was an expectation of an act of deliverance by God,
and on the other of a human Messiah who would be its
instrument. But Jesus is at once the God who performs the
act of deliverance and the Man who is its instrument. So
He appears as the one in whom the two paths presented by
sacred history converge, as being at once He who acts, He
who is the instrument of action, and He in whom God's
action is carried out. Thus Christ's position is defined by
His relationship with this twofold path in the Old Testament, within the twofold movement which composes it.
This throws a striking light upon the meaning of the
Incarnation. He is the action of God coming towards man
to save him and lead him to the Father. In Him, therefore,
is revealed the fullness of the mystery of God's love. But
He is also the Man who, raised up by God, mounts towards
the Father and thus fulfils the vocation of man. He is at
once—let us repeat—the movement of God towards man
and the movement of man towards God.

This is made clear in the other mysteries of the Old
Testament. We shall select three of the most important.
St. Paul in the Epistle to the Romans writes of Adam that
he is the type (typos) of him who was to come.[2] Already
this analogy is charged with extraordinary richness. As
Adam is the firstborn and the beginning of humanity, so
Christ appears as founding a new humanity. It is an aspect
of theology which is expressed by parallelism, throwing a

[1] See Jean Daniélou, *Essai sur le mystère de l'histoire*, pp. 181–201. [2] Rom. 5 14.

remarkable light on the mystery of the Incarnation itself. The Incarnation is the expression of the fact that Christ at the same time inserts Himself into the continuity of the human race, since He derives His flesh from Mary, and is likewise a new beginning, a new Adam, whom the power of God alone brings forth within that race.

Already we see what this analogy of Christ and Adam reveals about the fact of Christ. On the one hand, it shows us a mode of action appropriate to God alone, placing us in the midst of sacred history. For it is characteristic of the ways of God to create. And it is the same creative Word who formed man at the beginning of the virgin Earth, who comes in the fullness of time to restore Adam—still God's creature despite his unfaithfulness—and who fashions him anew in the Virgin's womb. Thus between the creation of the first Adam and the Incarnation of the last Adam an analogy is revealed which gives the Incarnation its theological dimension. The virgin Motherhood takes on its significance in the story of salvation. And the analogies which some have sought for this in the pagan religions now find themselves completely out of court. Nothing here has any connexion with the virgin mothers of Chanaanite cults or the loves of Zeus in Greek mythology. From the outset, the story of Christ is placed in a scheme of things which is its own, and which is neither that of mere human history, nor that of mythological fiction, but the supremely real scheme of the *magnalia Dei*, the works of God.

This is the fullness of faith. For the object of faith is not to believe in the existence of an inaccessible God, known only through symbols and myths. Religion would be sufficient for this. But faith is the belief in divine acts, in a God who intervenes in human life and reveals Himself in it by performing works which He alone is able to perform. By relating the conception of Christ to the creation of Adam, the New Testament and Tradition acknowledge its meaning as a historical act arising from sacred history, and enable us to place it in its proper order. They remove it from the realm of the merely factitious, from the realm of mere happening. But even so, they do not relate it to the categories of natural religion. They inscribe it within the continuity of a historical process in which one and the same God reveals Himself by modes of action which are one and the same.

At the very same time that the parallelism of Christ and Adam is teaching us something of the divine aspect of the Incarnation, it is also disclosing its human significance. In Christ is found the humanity which God willed to create in the beginning, whose development was hindered by the appearance of sin. In Him is revealed the final meaning of man's destiny. At the outset man was brought by God into Paradise, which signifies the sphere of divine life. So the meaning of human destiny appears. If the act of creation teaches us that God is Love, the entry into Paradise reveals that God comes seeking for man to raise him up to Himself. We see here the spiritual destiny of man in the strict sense of the word, that is, his call to be transfigured by the Spirit of God.

Now this is to be fully accomplished in Christ. It is in Him that a divine Person is to take hold of human nature so as to unite it with Himself in a fashion so intimate that no closer bond could be imagined. As the conception of Christ renews the loving act of the Creator God, so the ascension of Christ instals human nature finally in the realm of the Divine. The word of Christ to the good thief: 'This day thou shalt be with me in paradise,'[1] means that the fiery sword which denied to sinful mankind any access to the divine life is henceforth withdrawn, and that the way is once more open to the sanctuary where 'Jesus Christ, our escort, has entered already.'[2]

So just as the creation of man related to the mystery of God, the entry into Paradise relates to the mystery of man. The first teaches us what God is—and He is Love. The second teaches us what man is—and he is holiness. The creation is the action of God coming to seek for man, and Paradise is the exaltation of man into the realm of God. But both are the work of one and the same Word. For the abyss that divides God from man cannot be crossed by man. God alone was able to fill up that abyss and come searching for man, in order to raise him above himself and bring him into the Father's house.

There remains, however, a further characteristic to add to this Adamic Christology which not only admits of harmonies, but also of contrasts. Paul stresses this: 'As it was through one man that guilt came into the world . . . all the more lavish was God's grace, shown to a whole multitude, the free gift he made us in the grace brought by one man, Jesus Christ.'[3] As sin followed the entry of the first Adam into Paradise, so forgiveness of sin precedes the restoration of the second Adam to Paradise. If it is legitimate to see, with Louis Bouyer, a parallel between Christ and Adam in Philippians 2 [8-9]: 'He lowered his own dignity, accepted an obedience which brought him to death, death on a cross. That is why God has raised him to such a height,' this contrast is rich in theological implications.[4]

---

[1] St. Luke 23 [43].   [2] Heb. 6 [20].   [3] Rom. 5 [12-15].
[4] Harpagmos, *Mélanges Jules Lebreton*, I, pp. 280–88.

For Adam was created in the image and likeness of God, that is to say, at once as lord of creation (since he is God's image), and as himself a creature (since he is only God's likeness). Six days were allotted to him to declare his sovereignty over the world, and the seventh day to acknowledge the sovereignty of God. But he did not give God the glory which was His due, exalting himself and claiming to be equal with God. That is why the new Adam humbled Himself, and although He had the right to equality with God, He clearly did not cling to this equality. Against the love of self, carried to the point of despising God, He set the love of God, carried to the point of utterly despising self. And that is why He gave perfect glory to God, by becoming obedient unto death.

Thus the Adam sequence: creation, paradise, sin, is contrasted with the Christ sequence: Incarnation, Passion, Ascension. The mystery of the Cross comes to restore the damage wrought by the first sin. Opposite the tree of the knowledge of good and evil stands the tree of the Cross, which is the tree of life, to which in the end Adam has access: 'Who wins the victory? I will give fruit from the tree of life, which grows in the Paradise of my God.'[1] Opposite the first woman, disobedient Eve, stands the new Eve, the perfect servant of the Lord, whose heel crushes the head of the Serpent who seduced the first Eve. So all the knots are untied, and what was undone is done afresh within the same order.[2]

The typology of Adam showed the relationship of Christ with universal humanity, which is what the genealogy of Jesus indicates in St. Luke's Gospel by going back to the first man. The typology of Israel brings the Person and life of Christ into relation with the people of Israel and

---

[1] Apoc. 2 7.   [2] St. Irenaeus, *Adv. baer.*, III 22.

the mightiest of the works that God performed on its
behalf. With Israel we are deep in the history of mankind,
confronted by an intervention of the God who chooses,
saves, makes covenants, abides, outlining for a particular
people and on a lower level what is to be accomplished
in its fullness in Christ. The historical role of Israel seems,
indeed, not to be in any way connected with the nation's
natural qualities, but exclusively with the free choice by
which God called it to play a predominant part in the history
of salvation.

From the story of Israel let us consider the central
episode, the Exodus. This, too, appears to typify and
inaugurate the mystery of Christ in its wholeness, but under
new aspects. It is here without doubt that this reference
to the Old Testament reveals itself in all its richness as
something which shows forth the diversity of the aspects of
Christ. St. John points to Christ as the true Lamb who takes
upon Himself the sins of the world. And this throws a
remarkable light upon the meaning of Christ's Passion.
The angel of death was to strike all the firstborn. But the
houses of those who were marked with the blood of the
lamb were to be spared. So it is with Christ. The wrath of
God, which is likewise His holiness, is to destroy the sinful
world. But Christ takes upon Him the sins of the world
and bears the weight of God's wrath, so that those who
are marked with His blood should be saved. Thus Christ
appears at once in His divinity as the God who unites
wrath and pity, in His humanity as the Lamb who bears
the weight of wrath, and as the firstborn in whom mercy is
shown.

In the crossing of the Red Sea, it is under another aspect
that God's action is shown confronting the sinful world,
that of deliverance or redemption. What is essential in this

episode is the hopelessness of the position in which Israel finds itself. There is no human solution. And deliverance is the work of God alone. Now it is with this divine act that the New Testament compares the resurrection of Christ. He is the New Israel, the prisoner who is in a position of indescribable hopelessness, the hopelessness of death itself, delivered on Easter morning by God's power alone. But He is also the Word of God who on Easter morning, by the divine power that is in Him, awakens the resurrection within that humanity with which He remained united in a state of death. He is the Word of God who destroys the gates of hell and issues triumphantly from the tomb, henceforth opening the way of deliverance to all that believe. Christ is at once He who delivers and He who is delivered. He is also the New Moses, God's instrument, amongst His ransomed people, leading them towards the Promised Land.

St. John, who specifically relates the mysteries of Christ to the mysteries of the Exodus, shows us in Christ the heavenly manna, the true bread which came down from heaven. But the Synoptics, in the accounts of the temptation of Christ in the wilderness, point to Him as the New and true Israel who does not live only by bread, but by every word which comes out of the mouth of God.[1] Elsewhere St. John, in the Apocalypse, points to Him as the one who gives to the conqueror the hidden manna.[2] He is both the one who gives as the Word, the one to whom is given as Man, that which is given as God-Man.

The Epistle to the Hebrews, however, referring to the part played by Moses in making the Covenant on Sinai, points to Christ as Him through whose 'intervention, a new covenant has been bequeathed to us.'[3] And Christ

---

[1] Cp. Deut. 8 3; St. Matt. 4 3.   [2] Cp. Apoc. 2 17.   [3] Heb. 9 15.

Himself, at the most solemn moment of His life and in a text of unquestionable authenticity, is to take up as the sign and sacrament of the New Covenant the very sign of the first Covenant, while giving it an infinitely richer content: 'This cup is the new testament in my blood.'[1] Now, the Epistle to the Hebrews declares, 'Christ has taken his place as our high priest to win us blessings that still lie in the future. . . . It is his own blood, not the blood of goats and calves, that has enabled him to enter, once, for all, into the sanctuary; the ransom he has won lasts for ever.'[2] Christ takes up the action of Moses, shedding His blood upon the people and the altar, when He shares His blood with His disciples. But it is His blood that He shares, not the blood of goats and bulls. He is thus the one whose blood is shed, the victim who seals the Covenant. But He is also the God who makes the Covenant, and the people with whom it is made. In Him is fulfilled the New and true Covenant, since it is in Him that divine nature and human nature are bound together in a perfect and indissoluble sharing of life.

A final cycle is that of the Kingdom. Jesus is the true David, anointed not with the oil of unction but with the Spirit Himself, upon the day of His Baptism, according to the prophecy of Isaias about the Messiah born of the line of David.[3] This is testified in the account of the Annunciation: 'The Lord God will give him the throne of his father David; and he shall reign over the house of Jacob eternally.'[4] Yet the kingdom of which He is king is not an earthly kingdom, as He testifies before the legal representative of the people of Israel.[5] His rule is established not over a people of flesh, but over principalities and powers.

---

[1] St. Luke 22 [20].   [2] Heb. 9 [11-12].   [3] Isa. 11 [1].
[4] St. Luke 1 [32-33].   [5] St. Matt. 26 [64].

But He is at the same time the Kyrios, the Sovereign Lord. It should be noticed that the prophecies concerning the Messiah are just as rightly applied to Him, as are those concerning the eschatological Kingdom of God. He exercises the functions belonging to God. The Father 'has granted him power to execute judgement.'[1] We can see how these two paths merge into one another, by examining the passages in which Christ is called the Shepherd. The Old Testament proclaims at once that at the end of time God Himself will feed His flock, and that He will entrust it to a new David. The parable of the lost sheep and that of the Good Shepherd apply both these prophecies to Jesus.

St. Luke in his turn shows Him as the new Elias, the witness of God's ways, the prophet and worker of miracles.[2] He brings back to life the son of the widow of Naim, as Elias revived the son of the widow of Sarepta. He is persecuted by the leaders of His own people. And He is carried up into the heavens before the astonished eyes of His disciples, like Elias before the eyes of Eliseus. Thus is He found in the continuity of the Prophets of the Old Covenant. But He is also the one who reveals Himself to Elias, not in the storm, not in the burning fire, but in the gentle breeze of the Spirit. It is He, says St. Paul,[3] to whom the little Christian community remains jealously faithful, as Elias once was, left alone to defend God's rights. It is He by whose power the New Elias shall perform His works of power and might.

Finally He is the true Priest, of whom Aaron's priesthood was only an adumbration. For He is a priest after the order of Melchisedech. and thus unites in His sole Person the threefold ministry—royal, prophetic, and priestly—which

---

[1] St. John 5 [27].   [2] See Jean Daniélou, *Advent*, 1950.   [3] Rom. 11 [2-4].

follows three distinct paths in the Old Covenant. In this
He draws together all the charismata. The first Covenant
also had its priesthood, but it was only figurative. In other
words, it did not achieve its aim, but simply foretold it.
The proof of this is, as the Epistle to the Hebrews tells
us, that the high priest was only permitted to enter the
Holy of Holies once a year to offer blood of atonement.
But 'Christ has taken his place as our high priest to win
us blessings that still lie in the future . . . entered once for
all (ἅπαξ) into the sanctuary; the ransom he has won lasts
for ever.'[1]

But if He is high priest, He is also the Temple and He
who dwells in the Temple. Dwelling, or Abiding, means
in the Old Testament God's nearness to His people. It is
expressed by the presence of Yahweh in the Tabernacle
in the wilderness, then in the Temple at Jerusalem. The
Temple is the meeting-place of God and man, where God
reveals His will to His chosen, where man offers acceptable sacrifice to God. While drawing near to man, God
remains shrouded in mystery. The cloud that covers the
Tabernacle serves as the sign of this transcendence.
Similarly man could not bear the weight of God's glory
if it were displayed in all its majesty.

It is to this presence of Yahweh in the Tabernacle that
the New Testament refers in order to express that new
presence, infinitely more immediate, but nevertheless not
substantially other, which is the presence of the Word in
the Manhood of Jesus. 'The Word was made flesh,' St.
John is to say, 'and came to dwell (ἐσκήνωσεν) among us.'
And Matthew is to show us the glory of the Lord over-
shadowing Mary at the time of the Incarnation, signifying
that God's Dwelling is henceforth no longer the Temple at

[1] Heb. 9 [7, 11-12].

90

Jerusalem, but the Manhood of Jesus. 'Destroy this temple, and in three days I will raise it up again,' said Jesus Himself; and the Evangelist comments: 'But the Temple he was speaking of was his own body.'[1] Again, at the time of the death of Jesus the veil of the old Temple is rent, to show that it is henceforth the sanctuary where God dwells in a manner infinitely more intimate than in the sanctuary of the Old Temple. It is no longer golden seraphim that surround the ark of the covenant, but the heavenly liturgy that surrounds the Body of Christ wherein the Godhead dwells. And as the old tabernacle was the meeting-place of God and man, so the Manhood of Christ is henceforth the meeting-place of God and man, the means by which the prayer, worship and praise of man rise up to the Father: 'So that every request you make of the Father in my name may be granted you.'[2] Veiled in His lifetime by the appearance of the flesh, hidden beneath sacramental signs in the life of His Church, 'the glory of God . . . revealed in the features of Jesus Christ.'[3]

Many other themes might be examined which would lend themselves to similar development—those of Isaac and Jacob, Josue and Samson, Isaias and Jonas. We understand, then, as soon as we grasp its meaning, how Christ was able to expound to the disciples at Emmaus all that Moses and the Prophets had said concerning Himself.[4] For indeed it is true that the whole of the Scriptures speak of Christ. They are already a complete outline and foretelling of the Incarnation. They describe it in all its diverse aspects. And we see here yet once more the importance of referring to the Old Testament to increase our understanding of the coming of Jesus. Such a procedure sets it, by analogy,

[1] St. John 2 ¹⁹⁻²¹.   [2] St. John 15 ¹⁶.
[3] Cor. 4 ⁶. See Jean Daniélou, *The Presence of God (Le Signe du Temple)*, 1958.
[4] St. Luke 24 ²⁷.

within that order of being which the Old Testament reveals, and establishes it in the perspective of revealed ontology.

We said at the beginning of this chapter that the allusions of the New Testament to the Old Testament provided a context for the coming of Christ, related it to the unchanging ways of God, and thus offered us a basis for our faith. We can now see more clearly the meaning of this statement. The Incarnation appears to us not as an abnormal happening, but as the climax of a plan that starts at the beginning of history. For ever since then there is manifested to us a God who intervenes in human existence—and the Incarnation is to be His supreme intervention. From the beginning there is manifested the calling of man to share in the good things of God—and the Incarnation represents that complete sharing.

Either that, or else we must entirely reject the whole of sacred history, deny the whole supernatural order, throw away the entire Bible. But if we consider that the Scriptures bear witness to an order of reality which is difficult to reject *in toto*, we are compelled to agree that the Incarnation of the Word in Jesus of Nazareth cannot be anything but the absolute expression of the divine and of the human modes of being which are found throughout the whole of sacred history. It is in this way that reference to the Old Testament, the analogy between divine and human ways, provides a real demonstration, in the sense for which Irenaeus and Clement have provided the clue. If this demonstration is first of all valid for those who accept the Old Testament, it is also valid for those to whom the continuity of God's actions throughout the two Covenants appears to mark the boundaries of a region whose existence it is difficult not to recognize, even if its laws upset the claims of our reason.

. . . . .

At the point we have now reached, a question may well be asked. The mystery of Christ is that of a divine person taking on human nature. Now the Old Testament has shown us both divine actions and human persons. And it is certainly true that the New Testament brings us something entirely new when it shows us, as something achieved in the Person of Christ, the union of two paths which in the Old Testament were completely separate. But cannot we go further? Does not the relationship of the Person of the Word to human nature exist already before the Incarnation?

Two levels must be distinguished here. On the level of the Old Testament, it is difficult to say that we find a distinct conception of divine Persons. Without doubt we can speak of the Word of God, the Wisdom of God, the Spirit of God. But these are the powers of Yahweh. They do not appear as having any personal reality. On the other hand, from the very moment when the New Testament reveals for us the existence of Three Persons, it is clear that the Three Persons are already at work in the creation of the world and in the Old Testament. There is even more to be said. Within the Three Persons, it is the Word and the Spirit who are sent by the Father to carry out His hidden plans. Theology recognizes, therefore, that the Word has a special relationship with the creation of the world and man. Moreover, St. John already states this: 'It was through Him that all things came into being, and without him came nothing that has come to be.'[1] This recognizes His relationship with the Covenant made with

[1] St. John 1 ³.

Israel, for St. Paul shows us that the Word was already present in the midst of the people of Israel: 'The Rock that was Christ.'[1]

These implications of the Old Testament were developed by the Fathers of the Church, and they found their most complete expression in the theology of St. Irenaeus. The Incarnation is for Irenaeus the law of the history of salvation in its entirety. Now the Incarnation involves two aspects. It is God drawing near to man, and it is man drawing near to God. This drawing-near is to achieve its complete perfection in the Man-God. But it has already begun in the Old Testament. Or rather it begins with the creation itself, which is ordained for that purpose. So the Old Testament offers a twofold approach. On the one hand, it shows us the Word drawing near to man, 'becoming accustomed to him,' in a phrase dear to Irenaeus. Already in the Old Testament it is the Word who gives knowledge of the Father. This is one of the aspects of the presence of the Word in his *plasma*, in man who is His and who, even as a sinner, remains His creature.

Let us consider some texts in which the emphasis is placed on the presence of the Word among mankind. In the *Demonstration of the Apostolic Preaching*: 'All the different visions in the Old Testament represent the Son of God as conversing with men and living in their midst . . . It is not the Father of all—the world does not see him— it is not the creator of the universe who comes to speak to Abraham in this corner of the world. It is the Word of God, who does not leave mankind, foretelling what must come to pass and teaching men the things of God. It is he who went up and came down for the salvation of the afflicted, in order to deliver us from all idolatry. Thus the

[1] I Cor. 10 [4].

Word of God foreshadowed our ways and was accustomed to them, and so it is that he showed us in a figure what must come to pass.'[1]

Here Irenaeus takes up an idea of Justin, that of the appropriation to the Second Person of the theophanies of the Old Testament: 'The Son of God is sown everywhere among the Scriptures, now speaking with Abraham, now with Noah, giving him the measurements for the Ark, now seeking Adam, now judging the inhabitants of Sodom and showing himself to Jacob and leading him on his way, speaking to Moses out of the Bush.'[2] This fine passage sums up a collection of *Testimonia* on the theophanies of the Word. We find these *Testimonia* in the *Demonstration*. There Irenaeus refers to the appearance at Mambre, Jacob's ladder, the burning Bush. He adds the rock in the wilderness and the angel who appeared to Josue.[3] Here again Irenaeus follows Justin, who discusses on several occasions the appearance at Mambre (*Dial.*, LVI, CXXVI-CXXVIII). He devotes a chapter to the theophanies to Jacob (*Dial.*, LVIII), another to the burning Bush (LX). But we must recall that these texts are already applied to the Logos by Philo. It is, then, a theme of the theology of the first centuries. The originality of Irenaeus is not in his choice of passages, which is traditional, but in their interpretation.

The relevant point is the continuity which Irenaeus emphasizes between the presence of the Word among men from the beginning and the Incarnation: 'How could Christ be the end of the Law, if he was not its principle? He who brought on the end is also he who brought about the beginning. It is he who said to Moses: I have not been blind to the oppression which my people endure in Egypt

---

[1] 45; *Sources Chrétiennes*, 104.   [2] *Adv. haer.*, 4, 10. See 4, 7, 4.   [3] Josue 5 [18-14].

. . . and I have come down to rescue them[1]—he, the Word of God, accustomed from the beginning was to go up and come down for the salvation of those who were sick.'[2] This 'custom' is to reach its climax in the Incarnation properly so called, which is at once the 'custom' of God with man and the 'custom' of man with God: 'The Word was made the Son of man, to accustom man to receiving God and to accustom God to dwelling in man, according to the Father's good pleasure.'[3]

This is the answer to the Gnostics who divide Christ below from Christ above: 'They do not know that the Only Begotten Word of God is always present with the race of men, joined and mingled with his creature (plasma) according to the Father's good pleasure. Becoming flesh, it is he who is Jesus Christ. There is one Only God the Father and one Only Christ Jesus our Lord, who appears through the whole economy (dispositio) and recapitulates all things in himself. In this totality there is also man formed by God. Thus he recapitulates man in himself.'[4] So appears the unity of the work of the Word. He formed man; sinner that man is, He never ceases to hold him in His hand. At the end of time He takes hold of man again by His sovereign power in order to restore him to the Father.

We have noticed that, if in the Old Testament God accustoms Himself with man, in other respects man accustoms himself with God. At the same time, God comes down and man rises up. This ascent of man consists in his training by the Word, who accustoms him with God's ways as the Word is accustomed with man's. Thus the Old Testament, not only 'accustoms' the divine nature

---

[1] Exod. 3 7-8. [2] Irenaeus, loc. cit., IV, 12, 4.
[3] Ibid., III, 20, 2. [4] Ibid., III, 16, 1.

to being joined with human nature, it also prepares human nature for union with the divine nature. The training represented by the Old Testament is the rooting and grounding of monotheism in mankind. It is also the preparation for the Incarnation: 'God created man from the beginning by reason of His bounty; He chose the patriarchs for their salvation; He shaped His rebellious people by teaching them to serve God; He sent His prophets upon the earth, accustoming man to bear His Spirit, and to live in communion with God.'[1]

Now this preparation for Christ's Humanity by training humanity in the ways of God is precisely the typological meaning of the Old Testament. Irenaeus indeed continues: 'Thus the Word, passing through them all, ordained the building of the Temple, the choosing of the Levites, the sacrifices and offerings, not that He has need of anything: He is ever filled with all sweet smelling savour, but He was training a people who were always ready to turn to idols, teaching them through many a plea to persevere in God's service, calling them through secondary things to primary things, through figurative (typica) things to real things, through temporal things to eternal things, through fleshly things to spiritual things, according to His word to Moses: Thou shalt make all things in the likeness (typum) which thou hast seen upon the mountain. For forty days, indeed, he had learnt to understand the word of God and the heavenly characteristics and the spiritual images and the prefigurations of things to come.'[2]

Here we see the connexion between typology and pedagogy. Irenaeus teaches in a general manner that in the Old Testament God was thus making man familiar with His ways, accustoming him to them: 'Christ, from this

---

[1] Irenaeus, loc. cit., IV, 14, 2.   [2] Ibid., IV, 14, 3.

time forth, prefigured and foretold things to come through His patriarchs and His prophets, sharing by anticipation in the ways (dispositionibus) of God and accustoming His inheritance to obey God and to move through history as a pilgrim and to follow the Word and to pre-signify the things to come. Nothing indeed is empty or without significance in the works of God.'[1] Moreover, St. Irenaeus learnt his typology from the New Testament itself: 'Paul tells us: They drank of . . . the same prophetic rock which bore them company, the Rock that was Christ. . . . It is we that were foreshadowed in these events.[2] Through figures, indeed, they were learning to fear God and to persevere in His service.'[3] Typology, moreover, forms part of the Apostolic Tradition, one of whose features is to be the Christological interpretation of the Old Testament.

In this perspective, Christ appears as the fulfilment of all that comes before and after Him: 'The economy of the Lord is fourfold, and this is why four covenants have been given to the human race: one before the Flood, under Adam; the second after the Flood, under Noe; the third is the Law, under Moses; the fourth renews man, and recapitulates everything in itself; this is the Gospel.'[4] This shows Christ fulfilling human nature in Himself, in its concrete, historical reality.[5] It is by a similar approach that Irenaeus sees Christ reproducing the different ages of individual man: 'He penetrated all ages, being a child with the children, to make them holy, a young man with the young men, giving them His example.'[6]

By the term 'recapitulation' Irenaeus means the reality and fullness of the Incarnation of Christ in the race of Adam. But the term does not only mean that the Word

[1] Ibid., IV, 21, 2.   [2] I Cor. 10 4, 6.   [3] Irenaeus, loc. cit., IV, 14, 31.
[4] Ibid., III, II, 8.   [5] Scharl, *Recapitulatio Mundi*, p. 21.
[6] Irenaeus, loc. cit., 11, 22, 4.

has assumed manhood completely. It also denotes that He has become the Head of all men in such a way that it is the human race as a numerical whole which is substantially saved in Him. This is the Pauline view of recapitulation: 'There is only one Lord Jesus Christ, appearing throughout the universal exonomy and recapitulating all[1] in Him. In this totality man, the image of God, is included. Accordingly He recapitulates man in Himself, the invisible made visible, the incomprehensible made comprehensible, the impassable made passable, the Word made man, gathering together all things in Himself, so that, as the Word of God is at the head of the supra-celestial, spiritual, invisible world, so He has the Sovereignty of the visible and corporeal world, assuming in Himself the primacy, and whilst He places Himself at the head of the Church, He attracts all men to Himself when the hour is come.'[2]

It is because the Word recapitulated in Himself the man formed by God, that by virtue of the power which is His, He who is already the Head of the whole creation becomes in a new sense the Head of the human race, attracting all men to Him, concentrating in Himself, as Père Sagnard well says, all the generations of men.[3] Here we are confronted by a second group of texts in which the same themes recur: 'The Word of God is the Creator of the world. It is He, Our Lord, who in these last days is made man, showing His presence in the world, He who by reason of His invisible reality contains all that has been done and is implanted in all creation, as Word of God disposing and governing all things. And He has come visibly into His own, and He has been made flesh, and He has been hanged on the tree, so as to sum up all things in Himself.'[4]

---

[1] Cp. Eph. 1 [11].   [2] Irenaeus, loc. cit., III, 16, 6, citing St. John 12 [32].
[3] Irénée de Lyon, Contre les hérétiques, III, p. 293.   [4] Irenaeus, loc. cit., V, 18, 2.

Recapitulation concerns first of all every generation of mankind: 'He recapitulated in Himself the long series of mankind, and achieved salvation for us epitomized in His flesh.'[1] This remarkable text shows how Christ as Head fulfils substantially in His Person, which is the epitome of man, the salvation of the long series of human generations. And this recapitulation extends to all peoples: 'Luke shows how the genealogy that runs from Our Lord to Adam comprises seventy-two generations, through which He joins the end to the beginning. Thus Luke stresses the fact that it is Jesus who has recapitulated in Himself all the scattered peoples since the time of Adam, all the languages and generations of men, including Adam himself.'[2]

But this recapitulation not only relates to all past generations, it is also the installation of the glorified Christ as Head of the Church, and as the source of all spiritual life. The link between the word 'recapitulation' and the conception of Christ as Head (κεφαλή) of the mystical Body is well shown in the following passage: 'He recapitulated (these things) in Himself, uniting man with the Spirit and breathing the Spirit into man; He Himself became Head of the Spirit, assigning to the Spirit the Headship of man; it is through Him that we see, and hear, and speak.'[3] This text is to be taken with another: 'Over all there is the Father, and He is the Head of Christ; through all there is the Word, and He is the Head of the Church; in all there is the Spirit, and He is the fountain of living waters.'[4]

Finally, it must be added that this recapitulation of all things under the sole Head, who is the Incarnate Word, not only concerns man. It extends to the whole cosmos

---

[1] Ibid., III, 18, 1.   [2] Ibid., III, 22, 3.
[3] Ibid., V, 20, 2.   [4] Ibid., V, 18, 2.

of spirits and bodies: 'He has capitulated in Him all things, those that are on the earth and those that are in the heavens. But those that are in the heavens are spiritual, those that are on the earth are the "economy" relating to man.'[1] Irenaeus sees the figure of this universality of the saving act of Christ in the four dimensions of the Cross: 'As He is Himself the Word of God Almighty whose invisible presence is poured out upon us and fills the whole world, He still continues His influence upon the world in all its length, breadth, height and depth, for by the Word of God all is under the influence of the redeeming economy, and the Son of God was crucified for all, having traced the sign of the Cross upon all things.'[2]

Through recapitulation, that is, the gathering together of all things under His sole authority, Christ is the Universal King: 'According to the promise of God, an eternal King has arisen from the seed of David who sums up all things in Himself.'[3] This universal Kingship will be revealed in the Parousia when Christ shall raise up all flesh and judge every creature: 'The Church believes in the coming of Christ in glory to recapitulate all things and raise up all flesh belonging to the human race, in order that before Christ Jesus Our Lord, God the Saviour and King, according to the good pleasure of the invisible Father, every knee shall bow, in heaven, on earth, and in hell.'[4]

. . . . .

Thus for Irenaeus the Manhood of Christ is the mysterious centre of God's creation, the focal point upon which all converges, the bond of unity for earthly things and heavenly things. For it is through His Manhood that all glory rises to the Father. Christ's Humanity is beyond all

---

[1] Irenaeus, loc. cit., V, 20, 2. [2] *Dem.*, 34.
[3] Ibid., III, 21, 9. [4] I, 20, 1.

the greatness of Creation. For it springs from an order of religious greatness, that of holiness. It is in itself alone a universe greater than the universe. And when the universe shall pass away, this will remain for ever the object of the contemplation of the saints. This is as much as to say that to gaze into its unfathomable riches is the highest task of the human mind.

BIBLIOGRAPHY

L. Göppelt, *Typos, die typologische Deutung des Alten im Neuen*, Leipzig, 1959.

J. Daniélou, *From Shadows to Reality*, London, 1960.

Saint Irénée, *Demonstration de la prédication apostolique*, Paris, 1959. *The Demonstration of the Apostolic Preaching*, London, 1920.

Saint Hilaire, *Traité des Mystères*, Paris, 1947.

J. Gubomont, *Le lieu des deux Testaments selon la théologie de saint Thomas*, Bruges, 1950.

CHAPTER IV

PHILOSOPHY AND CHRISTOLOGY

In our attempt to place the fact of Christ in a context such as the Church and the Gospel provide, the New Testament itself has directed our attention towards the Old Testament. The fact of Christ springs from an order of its own, which is not that of science or philosophy, but is rather that of the history of salvation. So we have placed the fact of Christ in its relationship with that history, that is, in its relationship with a complete interpretation of existence. This is what, strictly speaking, constitutes biblical theology, which is a science whose principles are revealed, but which has a universal significance.

All the same we have not said that the fact of Christ was not capable of being the object of inquiry by the human mind. Only that inquiry can be of two different kinds. On the one hand, the history of thought presents us with a number of attempts to reduce the fact of Christ to a purely rational explanation. This is particularly what we find in German idealism. We shall choose for discussion the most recent attempt of this kind, that of Henry Duméry in his book, *Théologie de la Religion*. We shall then see that another attitude is possible, which, recognizing the impossibility of reducing the fact of Christ to a rational explanation, and accepting it as such, nevertheless admits that the mind works upon it in order to understand more clearly its meaning, its implications, its unity. This attitude is that of theology. We shall see what were its early approaches and what are the important problems which it has to face.

· · · · · ·

M. Duméry's attempt is to bring critical inquiry to bear

on the data of religion, so as to clarify the meaning of the symbols and concepts which the human mind is compelled to use to express a reality that by its very nature transcends its categories. This attempt would be quite valid if it were confined to clarifying the meaning of religious symbols, within their irreducible content, by freeing them from the inevitable anthropomorphisms in which they are clothed. But M. Duméry goes further. His reductive method, while claiming to safeguard the transcendence, actually reduces it to a rational explanation and the very object of his study finally disappears.

The essential quality of the Christian Revelation, in so much as it is to be distinguished from the various religions, is, as we have shown, that it deals with historical interventions of God, of which the chief is the Incarnation. These facts are reported in Scripture in their rough state, and the function of criticism is to apply itself to this aspect of them. This is precisely the role of theology, which is an exercise of the reason upon that special datum which is the history of salvation, the proper content of the Christian faith. Now M. Duméry does not appear to admit this. For him, Christianity is made up of a collection of schemes and categories which must be reduced to the requirements of the mind. This reduction is for him precisely the task of the philosophy of Christianity.

Let us quote our author here: 'The critical method can only be an immanentist method. . . . The immanentist method demands that reason should have jurisdiction over religion, and consequently regards it as homogeneous with man's other activities. . . . Argument from authority remains heterogeneous in relation to the arguments of reason. . . . The immanentist method appears as the rejection of all particularity. It is opposed to the various attempts to limit the power of reason from outside by dividing human reality into separate spheres of influence. It is a defence of rationality and intelligibility. On this basis it gives validity to an imperative which is indistinguishable from philosophical necessity.'¹ As for theology, 'it is the scence of religious salvation, it is not the science of speculative discrimination, of purely rational reflection.' Hence 'all that the theologian can tell the philosopher about the Trinity is its dogmatic value, its religious meaning, its soteriological significance; but not its critical structure, its formal coherence, its mode of judgement.'²

This position, whatever M. Duméry may claim, completely disposes of the Christian datum. Theology for him is a practical science of salvation, without speculative value; for him, it is the philosophy of religion that alone provides the rational criticism of Christianity; and it effects this criticism by showing that in Christian dogmas there are definitions created by the mind for the purpose of exploring the Ineffable One. We say the opposite: the philosophy of religion, in so far as it has for its objective a rational reduction, ends by showing that the Christian datum refers not to a demand of the mind, but to the authority of a Revelation. Its criticism consists in establishing the rational legitimacy of that authority. But it is the characteristic function of theology, which is a speculative form of knowledge, to elaborate upon the datum of Revelation by means of the reason. It has to criticize thought-forms which are its own creation not with reference to the requirements of the mind, but with reference to the requirements of Revelation itself.

We shall notice here a statement which reappears continually in M. Duméry's book. He claims that his criticism

¹ H. Duméry, *Critique et Religion*, pp. 50–51.   ² Ibid., p. 110.

105

of religion applies only to religious formulations and not to religion itself. But—his aim is really a metaphysical one, and is not only concerned with the criticism of knowledge. He speaks not only of formulations of God and the intelligible, but of the very reality of both. And these are definitions not only inasmuch as they are formulations, but also inasmuch as they define a sphere of existence, namely that of the intelligible with which his *critique* is concerned. Consequently, in relation to the matter in hand, they are no longer mere definitions of a dogmatic pronouncement, but are the reality proclaimed by dogma inasmuch as they are definitions whose analysis is his self-imposed task.

M. Duméry applies this to various dogmatic statements. In *Critique et Religion*[1] he attacks Blondel for maintaining that the Revelation of the Trinity opens a path closed to pure reason. 'This,'[1] he says, 'avoids the difficulty. For it is a question of knowing how the idea of the Trinity developed. It must not be forgotten that it too was built up by rational means.' 'The Trinitarian scheme,' he remarks elsewhere, 'consists of the application of a logico-metaphysical structure to data of very different kinds. We are dealing with a formulation of the divine mystery with the help of something both ingenious and problematic. In these conditions it becomes obvious that the mystery itself lies beyond that problematic solution.'[2] So the Trinity is a scheme which requires reductions. 'God, as a mystery, remains beyond our grasp.'[3] And M. Duméry concludes, in a passage that reveals the essence of his thinking: 'For an affirmation to be valid from the rational point of view, it must be homogeneous (and this is not the case: because the factual here exists side by side with the

[1] p. 109.   [2] *Philosophie de la Religion*, 1, p. 201.   [3] *Critique de la Religion*, p. 110.

ideal). For it to be valid from the point of view of the religious attitude is what remains.'[1]

In this way M. Duméry does recognize the non-rational character of the Trinity. But instead of seeing in this the expression of its supra-rational character, irreducible to any rational analysis, that is to say as the vision of a strictly revealed datum, he sees in it merely the expression of an imperfect construction, which invites further analysis and whose only value is pragmatic. It could hardly be more clearly stated that dogmas are mere definitions created by the mind to explore an otherwise inaccessible mystery, and that created as they are by the mind, the mind must recognize them for what it intended them to be, that is, as schemes and categories, but as things which have no speculative value.

Rational analysis which, in M. Duméry's work, reduces to nothingness the reality of the Trinity as constitutive of the being of God, similarly disposes of the acts of the Trinity which constitute its economy, the plan of salvation, sacred history. The idea of divine interventions in time is repudiated by our author. For him, history springs from a schematization which must be analysed. In reality, Christian assertions about the Incarnation of the Word, Redemption as deliverance from sin, the outpouring of the Spirit, the Parousia to come—these are mythical schemes which must be reduced to their rational meaning. And this meaning shows that such formulations are the expression of eternal relationships between God and the mind.

Hence, for him, the Christian claim consists merely in the privileged character of the fact of Jesus. There is indeed a factual datum which intervenes, and therefore a historical progress. But this progress is merely that of the

---

[1] *Philosophie de la Religion*, i, pp. 201–2.

progressive discovery of true religion, in other words of the fundamental relation of man to God. After the crude ideas of primitive religion, after the progress achieved by the Jewish people, religion expresses itself in Jesus through ideas which critical analysis shows to be the expression of an inwardness and universality that are the demands of the spirit. Jesus is the religious Summit of mankind. And that is why true religion is defined in relation to Him.

Here Duméry's position recalls that of Bultmann. He, too, undertakes a demythologizing which is in fact, as Cullmann has shown,[1] an emptying of history, which sees in Christian beliefs—Incarnation, Resurrection, Parousia—the mythological expression of the relationship of man to God. There is this difference, however, that Bultmann does not claim to reduce these expressions to a rational religion, but sees in them the expression of a crisis. In other respects Bultmann attempts to isolate the fundamental Christian statement from formulations that seem to him to be ~~peripheral~~. *outmoded* Here Duméry wisely remarks[2] that the mind, necessarily expressing itself on all levels, cannot dispense with myths, and that the Gospel myths are in every way preferable to those with which people might wish to replace them.

But myths are what they are. What we call the Incarnation is not a new event by which a new relationship is established between the Word of God and human nature. Theanthropy is religion itself, that is, the eternal relationship of God and man, the presence of the One in the mind of man. But Christ is the religious man in whom this relationship found its perfect expression, in whom the intimacy of God and man, which exists eternally, is at last

[1] 'Le mythe dans les écrits du Nouveau Testament,' *Numen*, 1954, pp. 120–135.
[2] *Philosophie de la Religion*, I, 243.

truly accomplished: 'To believe is to maintain, on the basis of a series of facts (the story of Jesus), the intrinsic relation of the mind to God. It is to hold and declare that the attitude of Jesus manifested spiritual inwardness. It is to acknowledge that in the events of His life, the eternal mediation, immanent in the mind, is revealed.'[1]

Accordingly the Incarnation does not correspond to a new event, an act of God. It is the expression of an eternal philosophical truth. In any case, how could there be an act of God? For M. Duméry, the One is a stranger to the world of definitions. Not only did He not create them, he will not accept them. The idea of a divine intervention is unthinkable. There are no actions but human actions. It is the mind that creates and invents. And its inventions are only the expression of a non-temporal reality. All history returns to myth. Critical analysis has for its objective the very task of isolating eternal meanings from the dross of mere occurrence.

We are quite familiar with all this. It is the objection that Greek rationalism already made to the Incarnation. The idea that God comes among men seemed absurd to Celsus and Porphyry. History for them was the world of the contingent, and God He who is a stranger to the contingent. Rationally this is quite logical. And here is the Christian religion insisting that God was made man! This is indeed folly for the reason. But the question is, is it true? In every way it is a statement that cannot be reduced to the simple conception of a bond between the created spirit and the uncreated One.

If we had to place M. Duméry in relation to his master Plotinus, we should say that the only difference is that, for him, Christian dogmas which are merely the mythological

[1] Op. cit., II, p. iii.

expression of eternal truths, must not be eliminated, but understood. Thus Christianity is preserved whole. But it is preserved as an expression of philosophical truths on the imaginative level. The philosopher is the man who knows this. He does not condemn the simple believer, who knows the truth, but is incapable of criticizing the formulation through which he approaches it.

It would be easy to show how M. Duméry applies the same procedure to the other events which constitute the object of faith, such as the Redemption. The sin of Adam, which made the Redemption necessary, is not a historical situation from which man can only be delivered by redemptive action, but 'it is the mythical projection by man of his own guilt.'[1] 'It must be termed noumenal. In the last resort this means that man can only be rightfully restored to himself by acknowledging that he is divided against himself, against God, against other people.'[2] Thus original sin is a myth that must be reduced to metaphysical significance, in other words, to the expression of a constituent necessity of the life of the mind as such.

Hence it is the same with redemption: 'It is not the event as an event which saves,' writes Mr. Duméry, referring to 'Spinoza, who refused to enslave his mind to the idolatry of the historical. Outward things cannot be the basis or justification of inward things. These latter can, strictly speaking, only rest on themselves.'[3] Hence the death of Jesus as such is only a *hapax*. It must be reduced to the 'inward and spiritual as well as eternal' operation which it signifies, that is, 'to the mediation of the Word immanent in minds.'[4] It will be noticed that the *hapax* is reduced to the mere factitiousness of anecdotal history. It is not that M. Duméry is unaware of the difference between

[1] Op. cit., II, p. 193. [2] Ibid., I, p. 271. [3] Ibid., II, p. 63. [4] Ibid., I, p. 195.

Historie and *Geschichte*.[1] But *Geschichte* is for him meta-history, that is, no longer history at all, but 'the expression of immanent necessity.'[2]

The ideas of grace and faith, which M. Duméry studies at some length, call forth similar remarks. Grace is the expression of the fundamental relation of man to God. It means that the mind can only find self-fulfilment through the immanent presence of the One.[3] This is the expression of a metaphysical truth which M. Duméry throws into sharp relief. But is it this ontological relationship that Christianity calls grace? In fact it means something quite different by that word, namely, the opportunity of sharing in the life of the Trinity which exceeds absolutely the requirements of the mind. But for M. Duméry this conception of grace is a scheme which must be reduced to the necessary and immanent relationship of the mind to the One.

We continually find the same reversal of viewpoints. What Christianity regards as a gratuitous event, a free decision of God's Love, which is not to be reduced to the demands of the life of the mind as such, is taken in the opposite sense by M. Duméry as a mythical scheme which is no more than the expression on a lower level of requirements integral to the life of the mind. Thus theology must be reduced to philosophy. But this is to throw away precisely that which constitutes the specific character of the Christian message, to reduce it to a collection of myths, perfect myths they may very well be, but myths all the same, whose ultimate meaning philosophy alone can provide for us.

We may say as much of faith. This is defined as the profound attitude of the religious man.[4] It differs from

[1] Ibid., II, p. 25.　　[2] Ibid., I, p. 271.　　[3] Ibid., I, p. 283.　　[4] Ibid., II, p. 38.

purely rational activity because 'it embraces all levels together,' that is to say, it finds its expression at one and the same time on the level of myth, on the level of ritual, on the level of feeling, and finally on the level of classifications. But faith in the biblical sense is something quite different from the religious attitude as such. It is to adhere to assertions which cannot be reduced to rational necessities, and which derive their certainty from the authority of the Word of Revelation. It is obvious that this appeal to authority would seem to M. Duméry to arise from extrinsic formulations which must be 'reduced.' And all at once it is faith itself in its specific character that is eliminated.

This is clear from a note in which M. Duméry explains that 'it is difficult to find a place for *auctoritas Dei revelantis* in the phenomenology of faith.'[1] The reason for this is 'that the act of the revealing God is expressed in a sociological scheme—authority. This scheme seems too extrinsic, when it is a question of the intrinsicality of truth or charity.'[2] Here again, however, M. Duméry is seeking to detach what that scheme itself might express, which is divine veracity, the faithfulness of God to Himself. This reduction leaves entirely on one side what is really in question, namely, not the truth of God as the ultimate foundation of all truth, but the fact of a historical revelation and the mind's commitment to it.

. . . . .

Thus the attempt to reduce the Christian deposit to a symbolization of a rational attitude, appears to be illusory. In fact it is not an understanding of the Christian deposit, but causes the very reality of it to disappear, and consequently can scarcely help us to understand it better. But even so, this does not mean that the human reason is not

[1] Op. cit., II, p. 148.   [2] Ibid.

to be applied to that deposit. This is the whole problem of theology. Indeed, the biblical point of view which we have reached so far is not enough. For the essential character of the biblical perspective is for it to be a concrete perspective, firmly settled within the realm of the facts of the history of salvation. But these facts are capable of various interpretations and need to be properly determined. They contain implications which must be distinguished. And this is where the intellect comes in.

To regard such discussions as mere theological quibbles would be to ignore the serious task with which they are concerned. We have already said that Christ appears to every man as an inescapable datum face to face with which he must make up his mind. But it must still be discovered in what that datum consists. Faith is not merely a religious experience, an affective shock, however profound. It is the commitment of the mind to an objective reality. And that reality without question surpasses the understanding. When we have said what we can about it, we must add that what we say falls short, by comparison, of what it is. Yet it still remains true that what we say of it is either true or false, and that it is impossible to say something of *no* account, for whatever is said means *something*.

Christ constitutes an order absolutely apart. Hence we understand that intellect advances gropingly and fails at every step. But through this obscure progress, something nevertheless becomes clear. It is through facing various points of view that certain truths may be distinguished. These points of view are, at first, partial. They only emphasize one aspect. A kind of dialectic therefore develops, through which the formulation of thought moves forward. One could say that our present task is to distinguish the meaning and ingredients of the history of this dialectic. For if certain formulations spring from the needs of a particular period, like the use of this or that word, the fundamental attitudes retain a permanent value, and we are always brought back to them.

Face to face with the Gospel datum, one early possible reaction was to misunderstand the essential 'novelty' of Christ. It consisted of seeing in Him a human personality who had been the object of a pre-eminent choice of God's. The analogy of the Old Testament favoured this interpretation, for it presented a series of men elect, of Messiahs, chosen by God, anointed by the Holy Spirit and endowed with divine power and wisdom to be the instrument of His mighty works. Such were Moses and Elias. Christ Himself appeared in their wake. But there was a danger of stopping short at this aspect. Without question, His election had a more pre-eminent, indeed an incomparable, character. He was not only a prophet, He was the Prophet, He who set a limit to the Revelation of God and who made known the Last Things. In Him absolute religion was fulfilled. He represented the highest religious summit of the human race. But He was only a man, although the greatest.

This conception was very widespread in the early days of Christianity. It was first of all that of certain Jews who believed in Christ as an authentic prophet, but did not acknowledge Him as the Son of God. We find a particular expression of it in *The Preaching of St. Peter*, in which we meet the doctrine of the true Prophet whose successive manifestations are Adam, Moses, Elias and finally Jesus. Jesus is the true Prophet. He is the Prophet's supreme manifestation. But He is only a Prophet.[1] It will be noticed that this doctrine is one which we are to find again in Islam. And Islam may perhaps have received it from the Judaeo-

---

[1] See Jean Daniélou, *Théologie du Judaeo-christianisme*, pp. 68–76.

Christians of Trans-Jordan with whom Mohammed was in contact. And it is also the doctrine of certain Jews to-day, who claim Christ as the glory, indeed the highest glory, of their race, but only as a great prophet: 'I did not see him raised,' writes Edmond Fleg.

This conception may have subtler forms, like that which we encounter in Gnosticism. Here it is no longer a conception of Transcendence and the unity of God that prompts the misunderstanding of the divinity of Jesus. It is, on the contrary, a mythology that divides the world into various levels of reality and so distinguishes a multiplicity of realities in Christ. There is the Only-begotten, the First-born, who belongs to the world of the pre-existent Pleroma. There is the Christ who is another aeon, brought forth on the occasion of the descent of Wisdom into the lower world to save it. There is finally the man Jesus, on whom Christ descends at the time of the Baptism under the appearance of a dove, and who is the prophet who lived in Galilee. Between these various persons there are correspondences. Each of them is a projection of others on different levels.[1] But there could be no unity between the earthly Jesus, a stranger to the higher world, and the Only-begotten of the Pleroma.

Conceptions of this kind were too radically at variance with the Gospel datum to be able to take root. But more moderate forms could exist. This is what we find in a number of authors, of whom the chief is Paul of Samosata. For him Christ is a man, the mere recipient of an adoption by God which places Him in an altogether outstanding position with regard to the salvation of men. It is not a question of simply seeing Christ as a prophet. His death and resurrection are acts which God performs through Him,

[1] See F. M. Sagnard, *Le gnose valentinienne et le témoignage de saint Irénée*, p. 185.

and which have absolute value. But it remains true that between the God who acts through man and the man who is God's instrument, there is a radical distinction, not only of nature but of person. The Person of the Word uses the Person of Jesus as a minister. There are two Sons of God: the Only Son, the Firstborn eternally begotten; and the adoptive Son, who is associated with the Only Son by a special choice made at the time of the Baptism in Jordan.

Here we can see the problem clearly. It is not a question of denying that in the Gospel datum there are two distinct realities. There is the Word of God, and there is the Manhood of Jesus. But it is the connexion between these two realities that is difficult to define. And it is just that connexion, in other words, that which makes Jesus true God and true Man, that was the new reality of the New Testament. For Paul of Samosata, the Word of God on the one hand, and the Person of Jesus on the other, if they are closely associated, yet remain separate. The two lines running through the Old Testament continue without meeting. We are still in Judaic Christianity. The proper order of the New Testament, at once the supreme work of the Trinity and the divine Person of Jeus, is left on one side.

The error of Paul of Samosata was to make Jesus a
+ human person whom the Word used merely as a minister. It necessarily provoked a reaction in the opposite direction which went too far in its turn, that of Apollinarius of Laodicea. In substance the reaction of Apollinarius was valid. He was returning to the great theological tradition of Alexandria. Clement of Alexandria, Origen, Athanasius, had concentrated their whole conception of Christ upon the fact that He was the Word of God who had taken flesh. This was what St. John had said: 'The Word was

made flesh.' The Incarnation appeared in the continuation of the mighty works of God in the Old Testament. It represented their supreme expression. The Word came to take the flesh which He had formed in the beginning to give it life by the power of the Spirit.

In his desire to show that Christ had no other personality than that of the Word, Apollinarius went too far. If we must define precisely the trend of his thought, we must say this: Apollinarius rightly maintained against Paul of Samosata that Christ is a unique nature, a φύσις. The expression was accepted. It was to be taken up by Cyril of Alexandria. It meant that there is but one subsistent reality in Christ. But Apollinarius in other respects gives the word φύσις its Aristotelian meaning as a principle of operation. Hence to say that there was only one φύσις in Christ means that there is in Christ only a single principle of operation, which is the Logos. Now in the ordinary case of man it is the soul which is the principle of operation. Apollinarius accordingly maintains that it is the Logos which in Christ takes the place of that principle of operation which is the soul, and thus that Christ has no soul, but is made what He is by the Logos acting in His body.

This statement of Apollinarius, which did violence to the Manhood of Christ, was bound to lead to a general reaction. This took different forms. Some theologians, like the Cappadocians, preserve what is fruitful in the Alexandrian doctrine of the Logos taking flesh so as to divinize it, but assert, against Apollinarius, that by 'flesh' must be understood human nature as a whole, including soul and body. Others, like Theodore of Mopsuestia, rightly emphasize the theological reasons for the integrity of Christ's human nature—the necessity to put on the whole man in order to save the whole man, and the part played by

Christ's human freedom in the work of salvation. But Theodore, in his turn, pushes the reaction far too far and seems to recognize in Christ a human person, subject to human actions, and he thus fails to recognize that it is the unique Person of the Word who is the subject of divine operations quite as much as of human works.

Theodore in his turn was later to be attacked by Cyril of Alexandria, who, giving Alexandrian theology its final expression, laid strong emphasis on the soteriological aspect of the Incarnation. The Word of God comes to save mankind. For this purpose He takes on human nature as the instrument by which He will reach the whole of the human race. The Incarnation is one aspect of a divine saving action which is displayed in the Passion, the Resurrection, the Ascension, Pentecost, the Eucharist, the Parousia. It is not only treated abstractly as an ontological structure, but also dynamically as an aspect of the pre-eminent action of the Trinity working out the salvation of the world through the Word and the Spirit. This theology was canonized by the Church at the Council of Ephesus, which condemned Theodore and his disciple Nestorius.

But if the Church at Ephesus recognized the value of the Alexandrian Christology, it corrected the vocabulary of Christology at the Council of Chalcedon. Cyril, indeed, kept the expression φύσις to denote the reality which constitutes Christ, and therefore maintained that He had a single nature, in other words that He constituted a single existent being. But we have seen that the expression was ambiguous, because φύσις is capable of being understood to mean the principle of operation, and that in this case it seemed to question the integrity of Christ's human nature. This is what Apollinarius had done. It is also something which some disciples of Cyril, like Eutyches, were not concerned to deny. So the Council of Chalcedon, uniting the vocabulary of Antioch with the theology of Alexandria, was to lay down that there are two natures in Christ, giving the word 'nature' the meaning of a principle of operation, and reserving the word 'person' to denote the unity of the existent being.

. . . . .

The Council of Chalcedon, while declaring on the one hand the unity of Christ as having His principle in the Person of the Word, and in other respects possessing the integrity of a complete human nature, laid the foundations of Christology. But it is obvious that this left in the air some serious questions about the right way to think of the relationship within Christ of His two natures. The Gospel has already raised this question. How are we to picture the exercise in Christ of His human activities? What communication is there between the two levels of existence where the unique Person of the Word lives and moves? How can we set side by side the unfathomable intimacy of the Word with the human nature that is His, and the unfathomable abyss that never ceases to separate the uncreated God from all created reality?

These questions first of all raise the problem of freedom, which seems to be the very expression of spiritual being. To acknowledge in Christ a created freedom quite distinct from His divine freedom is to start all over again and regard Him as a man who of His own free will cleaves to the divine will. On the other hand, to deny Christ this human freedom is surely to make Him a passive instrument—and to return to Apollinarius' error. What is more, this passive instrument is no longer a man. But if Christ is not a man, then the Incarnation is no longer anything but a word. And if the Incarnation is no longer a reality, our salvation is no longer a reality either.

Accordingly in Christ there is human freedom. But how are we to conceive its relation to divine freedom? If this human will is moved entirely by the divine will, then the whole idea of His freedom is nonsense! But that would be to misunderstand the nature of freedom, for freedom is not destroyed, but on the contrary fulfilled, by obedience to the will of God. In Christ, therefore, there must have been a perfectly constituted human will, one which never-theless was always lovingly obedient to the will of the Father. 'My Father loves me because I always do what pleases him.'[1] What is more, if there is no human will in Christ, all the value of the mystery of His Passion as a reparation disappears. For it is in His obedience as man that He makes reparation for that which the disobedience of Adam had destroyed. It is in His Manhood that He is the high priest who intercedes after the order of Melchise-dech—and this not only in the days of His earthly life, but established for ever as mediator between man and God.

We are now in a position to see why the existence in Christ of full human freedom concerns the very heart of the Christian mystery. It is because He is man in the full sense of the word that Christ was, in fact, able to be the perfect fulfilment of God's plan for man, leading human nature to the end for which God created it. For freedom is the distinguishing characteristic of man. It was through this freedom that man turned away from God. It is this freedom which, in Christ, cleaving to God in a perfect manner, makes reparation for sin and restores the Kingship of God. And this is first accomplished in the Person of

[1] St. John 8 ²⁹. (The author seems to have combined this text with St. John 15 ¹⁰. Trans.)

Christ, so that this Manhood, perfectly united with the Godhead, not only ontologically through the hypostatic union, but also actively through His voluntary obedience, should be at once the exemplary pattern of all sanctity and the first cause of all sanctification.

Thus it is that, according to the measure of Christ's perfect freedom, so was He able to give perfect glory to establish the final pattern of worship. For the glory of God is precisely to be freely loved. This is the essence of sacrifice, which is the acknowledgement of God's absolute sovereignty, and therefore the revelation of the infinite grandeur of God. This perfect sacrifice, of which pagan and Jewish sacrifices were no more than vague outlines, finds in the sacrifice of Christ its total and perfect fulfilment—a sacrifice offered in such a way that from henceforth all other sacrifices are abolished, and we ourselves cannot any longer offer to the Father anything other than perfect love. This perfect love is the love with which the only Son loved the Father; it is not only the eternal love with which He is united in the unfathomable depths of the life of the Trinity, it is the created love with which He loved, and still loves, through the human will which came to Him at the Incarnation.

We see, therefore, that the question of the human freedom of Christ is not a purely psychological question. And the practical exercise of this freedom will always remain a profound mystery. But its existence relates to the very heart of the faith. It springs from the important issues involved in the Creation and from the settled character of the work of God. It springs also from the important issues of the Redemption, which does not substitute a divine act for a human act, but is the divine act leading on the human act to its fulfilment. This, which is the completion of

God's work, is first accomplished in the very Manhood of Christ. In Him human nature reaches its full completion. And this completion could not be anything but the fullness of the exercise of a freedom which is united with God through love. By this very means the value of human liberty is guaranteed. Sanctifying grace, the extension of the grace of Christ, will not destroy the Christian's freedom, but will free it from its chains to lead it on to its fulfilment.

The nature of Christ's knowledge will soon present different problems, perhaps even more difficult ones. Here once again we must remember that the exercise of the reason is part and parcel of human nature. The infinite knowledge of the eternal Word does not, therefore, take the place of the human understanding of Christ in relation to those things which properly concern it. For it is this human mind, destined by God for the Beatific Vision, which Christ came to assume in order to lead it in Him to achieve its end, in such a way that every illumination of the human mind shall be a sharing in the Beatific Vision which was first realized by the Word in the human nature which is His own.

This raises the difficult question of the limits of Christ's human knowledge. Such limits seem indeed to be required by the Gospel. When Christ was learning the rudiments of Holy Scripture, His mind was acquiring in this way knowledge which it did not previously possess. This implies, then, that there were things of which He was ignorant. This ignorance belongs not to human nature as such, which can receive by the grace of God immediate knowledge of reality, but to the fallen state of human nature. As Christ submitted voluntarily to the suffering of human nature, so also He submitted to its other humiliation, which is ignorance. Otherwise it would have to be said that Christ pretended to learn what He already knew. And such a piece of play-acting would be unworthy. Christ pretended nothing. He did not pretend to be a man; he really *was* a man.

This shows the need to consider Christ not only in His abstract essence, but in His successive states and in the organic connexion between those stages. The Word of God comes to take up human nature in its fallen, darkened state, so as to lead it to His state of glorification and illumination. This is true of the different aspects of His human nature. In so far as the exercise of the reason in man's earthly condition is bound by the limitations of space and time, the Word of God willed that His human mind should share the condition of every human mind. And thus we are bound to admit the truth of His limitations, under pain both of misunderstanding the truth of the Incarnation and of denying the earthly life of Christ its character as a mystery of humiliation.

Here there are two levels of reality which are not always sufficiently distinguished. On the one hand there is the Manhood of Christ as it is fully realized in the glorified Christ. It is this Manhood which returns by right to the incarnate Word, and in which the effects of its union with the Word find their full meaning. It is totally withdrawn from mortality and suffering; it is totally beatified; it is totally illuminated. It is very much a question of Manhood in the most real sense of the word. In other respects there are earthly conditions, the flesh, which the Word assumed in humility and in which He wished to share the consequences of sin. It is on the level of that Manhood that certain limits appear as arising from the very mystery of His humiliation.

This shows us the point at which it becomes impossible

to dissociate the study of the essential 'being' of Christ from that of the states through which He passed. Or, if we wish to discuss the essential 'being,' we must speak of the glorified Christ. Numerous errors doubtless arise in this connexion from the fact that we take as our point of departure Christ as He appears in the Gospel. But in Christ as He appears in the Gospel there is a voluntary humiliation which deprives the Manhood of Christ of the privileges to which it is entitled—privileges which the Ascension plainly established as naturally His own. What is constant is the hypostatic union itself, which constitutes the being of Christ and all that follows of strict necessity. But there are in the glorified Christ privileges which He renounced in His abasement, and we must take account of this difference.

Thus, in the question with which we are dealing, we are led to consider three levels of existence in Christ. There is in Him the divine knowledge which comes to Him as the eternal Word; there is the human knowledge which the hypostatic union implies, and which is constituted by the Beatific Vision; and finally there is the human knowledge, which is bound up with the state of glorification of His Manhood, and which is completely renounced in His state of humiliation.[1] It is at this level that there is in Christ an ignorance whose object and limits must be strictly defined, but which justifies the statements in the Gospel where Christ makes it quite clear that He is unaware of certain realities.

Not only has Christ human freedom and a human mind, but He also has a human consciousness by which His Manhood is present to itself. This has been defined by the

[1] Most theologians recognize in Christ, over and above this, an infused human knowledge. This knowledge certainly belongs to Him by right. But it is permissible to suppose that the renunciation of the actual exercise of this knowledge is an aspect of Christ's self-humiliation.

Church in opposition to the error of Gunther who saw in consciousness the constitutive element of the person and hence admitted in Christ no other consciousness than that of the Word. But consciousness is not the person. It is, on the other hand, that which defines the mind as such, for self-consciousness is that which differentiates it from material beings. Christ would therefore not be truly man if there had not been in Him that which is the very property of man as mind.

But here arises a problem which in our own time has given rise to innumerable controversies, namely that of the relationship of Christ's human consciousness to His Divinity. Was Christ aware of being the Son of God? On the one hand His consciousness is a human consciousness, which is hence awareness of His Manhood, of which it is only the reflective aspect. And on the other hand, how are we to imagine that Christ in His Manhood could have been unaware that He was the Manhood assumed by the Word? Some people, like Père Galtier, solve the problem by (supposing) an illumination of Christ's human consciousness by the Beatific Vision. In this way Christ would be aware in His Manhood of His divine nature through a kind of external illumination. But do we not then run the risk of falling back into a kind of Nestorianism, of misunderstanding the fundamental unity of the Person of Christ?

In reality the problem that arises here is the equivalent on the gnoseological level of that which the hypostatic union presents on the ontological level. This has been strikingly expressed by Karl Rahner: 'Self-consciousness is the inward light of a being in actuality to itself, or to be more precise, in actuality to the subject which possesses this being-in-itself. It follows, therefore, that according to the strict requirements of scholastic metaphysics, it is false to say that the human soul of Christ had no knowledge of the hypostatic union except in the manner of knowing an objective fact. In proportion as the hypostatic union is a real ontological definition of the human nature, and in proportion as this human nature is something which exists in itself, so this union is bound to be a datum in the self-consciousness of this human nature.'[1]

These lines of approach are not only interesting inasmuch as they help to throw light on a difficult problem. They also have a methodological interest. They show, as Rahner himself says, that 'if there is an ontic Christology, there can also be an existential Christology.'[2] They also show that the mystery of Christ is a datum on which the human mind will always be compelled to exercise itself, without ever being able to exhaust its possibilities, yet ever revealing its riches. For even if there are statements that remain established—like the definition of Chalcedon, characteristic of what Rahner calls ontic Christology—other approaches may yet enable us, not to elucidate a reality which will always remain mysterious in its depth, but to formulate its other aspects correctly.

. . . . .

Our point of departure was the fact of Christ as the New Testament bears witness to it. This fact appeared to us in its uniqueness as raising a question from which it was impossible to escape, so decisive is it for the meaning of human existence. It appeared to us that it was impossible to reduce it to the categories of philosophy or religion, but that it confronted us with an event of a unique order. We then inquired whether this event nevertheless provided a certain context. And, basing ourselves on Christ Himself and His Apostles, we studied this context in the Old

---

[1] *Écrits Théologiques*, I, p. 142.   [2] Ibid., p. 144.

Testament. We concluded that we found ourselves face to face with a datum with a different bearing, but nevertheless of the same order, which already placed us in the realm of faith proper. Thus we arrived at the idea of a history of salvation, constituted by divine acts of which the coming of Christ constitutes the Summit.

It is in this perspective that we can now return to the New Testament. We approached it first on the level at which it arises in ordinary experience, where it appears to spring from the historical datum in the common meaning of the word. This is a preliminary phenomenological approach, which contents itself with describing the datum as it arises. This datum later appeared to offer analogies with another datum, that of the Old Testament, so that we arrived at general categories which show that we are here face to face with an order of reality having consistence, coherence and continuity. We must now return to the New Testament to reconsider the data in this new light, and examine their meaning in the total perspective of a history of salvation.

BIBLIOGRAPHY

St. Leo the Great, *Sermons*, 1, Paris.

St. Thomas Aquinas, *Summa Theologica*, 3ª, 16–36.

Pierre de Bérulle, *Discours de l'État and des Grandeurs de Jesus*, Paris, 1865.

Karl Rahner, *Écrits Théologiques*, Paris, 1959.

CHAPTER V

THE MYSTERIES

SACRED history is, throughout its course from Genesis to the Apocalypse, the history of the works of the Word and the Spirit. 'It was the Lord's word that made the heavens,' says the Psalmist.[1] And it is the Lord's word that shall bring the plan of salvation to its completion when, after vanquishing all His enemies, His kingdom shall be established for ever. 'I am before all, I am at the end of all.'[2] It is unduly to narrow our perspective only to consider the action of the Word during one period of cosmic history. It is coextensive with all times. 'At the beginning of time the Word already was. . . . It was through Him that all things came into being.'[3] And He who was is also He who is coming. His name is: 'I am coming soon' (ὁ ἐρχόμενος).[4]

But it remains true that there is a privileged period in this action of the Word in history which constitutes its centre, and around which everything is organized, so that what has gone before seems to be a preparation, and what follows seems to be an unfolding. This period is the one between the Incarnation and the Ascension. It corresponds to the earthly life of Christ. But the earthly life of Christ forms part of the mighty works of the Word of which it is the climax. Oscar Cullmann has well shown in *Christ and Time* the paradoxical character of the Christian theology of history, according to which the climax has taken place, the end promised by God is substantially attained; no event will ever have greater importance than the Resurrection of Jesus Christ.

. . . . .

The earthly life of Jesus is, as we were saying, a climax

[1] Ps. 32 6.   [2] Apoc. 1 17.   [3] St. John 1 1-8.   [4] Apoc. 22 12.

in sacred history, that is, in the mighty works of the Word. It is in this respect that the essential episodes in that life are mysteries. They are Trinitarian works which continue the works of God in the Old Testament, but are infinitely more important. For they are concerned with that new and supreme reality which is the human nature with which the Word is united, and the works which He accomplishes in and through that human nature. These works are divided into three cycles, the mysteries of childhood, the mysteries of the public ministry, and the mysteries of the Passion and Resurrection.

It is obvious that each of the mysteries in each of these cycles would need prolonged investigation, which could never in any case exhaust them. However, our purpose here is above all to present general truths. And that is why we shall devote only a few pages to this vast topic. First of all we shall notice that in the New Testament three elements contribute their dimension of mystery to the essential episodes in the life of Christ. The first is the intervention of divine Persons who reveal them as wholly divine works—and it is this that marks the mystery. The second is the typological or prophetic reference to the Old Testament, which places them in the perspective of sacred history. The third is the presence of the angels, which gives them their cosmic dimension by showing that they are concerned with the creation as a whole.

This is especially true of the mysteries of childhood. The first is that of the Incarnation itself. St. John has fixed for ever its theological expression: 'The Word was made flesh.' This divine act is that by which the whole Trinity accomplishes the union of the Person of the Word with a human nature taken from the stock of Adam. 'The Holy Spirit will come upon thee, and the power of the most

High will overshadow thee.'[1] This gives rise to that pre-eminent work which is the human nature of the Man-God, the supreme fulfilment of the Love of the Trinity in such a way that around His Manhood the rest of the creation is arranged in time and organized in space, the articulating principle of history and the sun of the universe, created reality, but the foremost of all created realities and worthy to be exalted above all created realities, 'high above all princedoms and powers and virtues and dominations, and every name that is known, not in this world only, but in the world to come.'[2]

We could stop to reflect upon the sublime qualities of Christ's human nature, established through His absolutely unique relationship with the Person of the Word in a state of total consecration which renders it infinitely holy. But the Incarnation also presents other aspects. What the Word of God comes to take up once more through the Manhood of His Person is that very Adam whom He formed in the beginning, who had escaped from the Father's hands, and whom He comes to take up again this time in a grasp so firm that he will never escape again, and so intimate that He establishes with him an incomparable covenant. The Incarnation thus appears as a moment in the history of the relationship between the Word and human nature, but it is the decisive moment, the supreme efficacious intervention, by which human nature is infallibly guided towards the end for which it was eternally destined in the secret counsels of the Trinity. From His conception the incarnate Word recapitulates in Himself the whole preceding history of mankind, as St. Irenaeus well says. He is already the First-born of a multitude of brothers.

In other respects, what the Word comes to take up is

[1] St. Luke i [35].   [2] Eph. i [21].

mankind in its fallen state. He comes to take hold of the
flesh in order to quicken it through the Spirit. And the
misery of the flesh was the consequence of the sin of the
spirit. Now Christ is without sin. Ever since He took
human nature, that human nature possessed as something
normal the glory of the Spirit. This is why the fact that
the Word was made flesh represents a mystery of self-
abasement, of humiliation. 'His nature is, from the first,
divine, and yet he did not see, in the rank of Godhead, a
prize to be coveted; he dispossessed himself and took the
nature of a slave.'[1] Thus the Incarnation places us from
the first in a world marked by sin. It is the first stage of the
Redemption, the first of the steps by which the Word of
God goes down into the abyss of misery, into the depths of
death, to free imprisoned man from death.

This pre-eminent act, as great as, and greater than, the
creation of the world, all the more so since its object is
of more importance than the whole world of bodies and
spirits, is essentially a work of the Trinity. The Spirit of
God rests upon Mary to give birth to the new creation,
as He rested upon the primaeval waters to give birth to
the first creation. The Power of the Most High over-
shadows her as He overshadowed the Tabernacle of the
Dwelling. Similarly the Dwelling of Yahweh is henceforth
no longer the Temple at Jerusalem, but the Manhood of
Jesus: 'The Word came to dwell among us.' But this
supreme work is a hidden work. It is concealed from the
eyes of the body; it is accomplished in profound obscurity,
in the silence of night. 'There was a hush of silence all
around, and night had but finished half her swift journey,
when from thy heavenly throne, Lord, down leaped thy
word omnipotent.'[2] Thus it prepares for the hidden works,

[1] Phil. 2 6-7.   [2] Wisd. 18 14-15.

but it blazes forth in the sight of spirits and of those who contemplate wisdom. It is accomplished amid the awe of the angels, who adore the Word of God in His incomprehensible humiliation.

The public life of Christ, more than the rest, might seem to take place at the level of human actions, and to belong more definitely to history in the ordinary sense of the word than to that of the *magnalia Dei*. Moreover, it is the period of His ministry that historians are most ready to isolate, rejecting what relates to the infancy and what follows the Passion as belonging to the realm of pure faith, and thus being of no further interest to them. Now, as we have said, nothing is more questionable than this view. The public life of Christ keeps us always in the midst of sacred history. Moreover, it is inaugurated by the theophany at His Baptism, when the Father bears witness to the Son, and the Spirit rests upon Him. Legions of angels surround the Word, as He Himself tells us. And yet, as we have said, the acts which He accomplishes are at the same time the acts of men, continuing those of Moses, David, and Elias, but also acts of God, continuing the works of Yahweh in the people of old.

In fact Christ's public life belongs to the excellent economy of the mighty works of the Word, as a time of preparation and anticipation. First of all its object is to establish the economy of the Church, which will become active and can only become active after the Resurrection, Ascension, and Pentecost, when the Spirit has been given. It is, above all, to this very order that the public life of Christ belongs, and it is this that explains so many astonishing paradoxes. For, considered only from the human point of view, it seems to be a failure. The teachings of Christ are understood by no one, not even by His Apostles. His behaviour arouses the antagonism of the leaders of His people, and finally His Passion is the supreme expression of this failure.

Men have often pondered on this problem. Is the unbelief of Israel the expression of the ill will and perversity of a few misguided leaders? Might it have been otherwise? Could Christ have succeeded? Guardini asks this question in *The Lord*, and gives an affirmative answer. Jules Isaac connects the unbelief of Israel with the hostility of political priests to Jesus. All this is beside the point. What Jesus taught could not have been understood, what He instituted could not have been accepted, what He was could not have been admitted. For all this belonged to an order to which alone the Spirit gives access—and, as St. John profoundly says, they did not understand because 'the Spirit had not yet been given to men.'[1] So we must understand the ministry of Jesus as the setting in order of a number of things which were only, and could only be, put into effect after His Resurrection, for they were the expression of something which had to spread among mankind, namely of something which would be substantially accomplished in the Resurrection.

The public life of Jesus, moreover, has a very special quality of anticipation. It is the pre-constitution of the Church. It springs from a wisdom which disposes all things in an ordered and harmonious sequence. Cullmann has well shown what an important place the idea of καιρός, of due season, occupies in the life of Christ. Everything has its καιρός which is fixed by the Father. And the Word, who is the perfect Servant, accomplishes the work that has been entrusted to Him by the Father, by following these successive stages. He is not like those men who have

[1] St. John 7 ³⁹.

no καιρόι, whose life is without meaning.[1] For Him, the periods of His life are so many stages in sacred history determined by the Father's will. Each has its proper content. There is a time to sow and a time to reap. Christ appears here as the Sower whose harvest the Apostles will gather.

This is first apparent in the fact that the greater part of His life is devoted to establishing the structure of the Church. This is undoubtedly one of the most astonishing features of His ministry. Christ seldom preached to the crowds. He did not go beyond the borders of Israel. But He laid the foundations of His Church. The first step was the choice of the Twelve, who were to be the Patriarchs of the new people, corresponding to the twelve sons of Jacob. Among the Apostles He gives the leading place to Peter, so that he may be the unshakeable stone resting on the rock that is Christ, a stone upon which the faith of the Church will repose, and on which it will be able to rely. Finally, He teaches the Apostles whom He has chosen, He tests their loyalty, He arms them with powers that will enable them to distribute to the world the fruits of the work which He is to accomplish in His Passion and Resurrection.

He teaches them—but they do not understand. They are shocked by Christ's talking in parables to the crowds 'because, though they have eyes, they cannot see, and though they have ears, they cannot hear or understand.'[2] To the Apostles, on the other hand, 'it is granted . . . to understand the secrets of God's kingdom.'[3] But this simply means that He expounds to them the meaning of what He explains to the crowds in a symbolic manner. For as to comprehending the inmost meaning of those secrets, the Apostles understand no better than the crowds.

[1] *Christ and Time*, p. 39 ff.   [2] St. Matt. 13 [13].   [3] St. Matt. 13 [11].

It is the Spirit alone, when He is given, who will teach them all things and recall for them all that Jesus had said.[1] So the position of the Apostles is no different from that of the crowds as regards their fundamental inability to know the secrets of the Kingdom, in so far as the Spirit has not been given. In this respect the crowds are not blameworthy any more than they are sinless. The only sin is to be the sin against the Spirit, in other words, the denial of the Spirit when He is given. Thus we see the meaning of the special teaching given to the Apostles. It simply refers to the preparation of their future mission. Christ arms them with a doctrine which they will understand later.

It is the same with the sacraments. Christ formally institutes them during His ministry, He makes them efficacious by His death and Resurrection, He causes them to be brought into use at Pentecost. Harald Reisenfeld has shown this in the case of baptism.[2] It is instituted by Christ in its ritual of water and its reality as Spirit. But as it is the sharing in the death and Resurrection of Christ, it cannot come into use until after the death and Resurrection. This is what Tertullian in his wisdom replied to those who raised the question whether Christ and the Apostles baptized during the earthly life of Christ, and whether the Apostles were themselves baptized.[3] The Eucharist, similarly, was instituted by Christ in the full reality of its signs and content by a mysterious anticipation of His redemptive action, in which, as Gregory of Nyssa remarks, He disposes of time in a sovereign manner,[4] but which was not to bring its sanctifying effects into action in the bosom of the Christian community until after the Passion and

---

[1] St. John 15 [26].
[2] 'La signification sacramentaire du baptême johannique,' *Dieu Vivant*, 13, pp. 27–45.
[3] *Traité du baptême*, 13, 2, *S.C.*, p. 85.   [4] *P.G.*, XLVI, 612, C-D.

Resurrection had given effective reality to the saving act of which it was the efficacious memorial.

But the anticipations that constitute the public life of Christ are not only concerned with the time of the Church, in which the grace of the Resurrection will sanctify souls, but also with the eschatological creation, in which the grace of the Resurrection will be spread abroad upon bodies too. So it seems that this period of the activity of the Word provides in outline the whole range of works which He will accomplish as a result in succeeding times. If the Old Testament was the advent of the New, the earthly life of Christ in its turn is the advent of the Church and Heaven. This is what Origen explains when he says that the Old Testament is the shadow (σκιά), the New Testament the image (εἰκών), and the Kingdom the reality (ἀλήθεια). The Church and Heaven are revealed in their turn as two successive stages, and the Church is to appear in relation to Heaven as advent to image.

This is verified in the case of an aspect of Christ's ministry which we have not mentioned, that of miracles. We have spoken of them so far as being an expression by Christ of the divine nature. But we must now consider them afresh in their significance as mysteries. Now the meaning of miracles appears in this context to be that of anticipations. They are primarily signs of eschatological Creation. They are an anticipation of the return to Paradise, in other words of a cosmos transfigured by divine energies and withdrawn from its biological condition. This is not a mythical dream, but the very substance of faith. For faith is, above all, faith in the resurrection, that is, in passing from death, from the state of misery resulting from separation from God, to life, that is, transfiguration by divine energies.

Now this is what is anticipated symbolically in miracles. They are only possible in a theological perspective, that of the action of the Spirit. They do not belong to the world of nature. On the other hand, they are placed in a world which is still that of nature. That is why they are so hard to place. They reveal that with Christ Paradise is henceforth restored.[1] But in other respects until the Parousia Paradise remains a hidden reality. Miracles are therefore an exception to the general rule of the history of salvation. They testify to an order which does not yet exist. But they are an anticipated manifestation of that order, destined to signify the object of the action of the Word in the diversity of its aspects and in the totality of its extension. Thus the works of the Word in the earthly life of Christ reveal potentially all that is to be unfolded later in the sequence of the history of salvation.

If miracles have primarily an eschatological meaning, they have also a sacramental meaning, because they are themselves anticipations of the various aspects which the action of the Word is to take in the sequence of history. Cullmann has shown, indeed, that in St. John the miracles of Christ contain references to baptism and the Eucharist.[2] Here, by a kind of reversal, they appear as material and imperfect outlines of what the sacraments perform spiritually and perfectly. The changing of water into wine at Cana prefigures the passage from a life of sorrows to a life of glory which will be brought about by baptism. The opening of the eyes of the man born blind prophesies the opening of the eyes of the soul which will be brought about by the baptismal illumination (φωτισμός). The multiplication of the loaves for the crowds in Galilee is a figure of

---

[1] See K. L. Schmidt, *Le problème du christianisme primitif*, pp. 50-51.
[2] *Les sacrements dans l'Evangile Johannique*, 1951.

the true bread that comes down from heaven to give life to the world: 'he who eats it never dies.'[1]

Thus, as the actions of the Word in the New Testament appear to be prefigured by the actions performed by that same Word in the Old Testament, they now appear to us as types of the actions which that same Word will perform in the Church and in the Kingdom. Hence the history of salvation is clearly shown as that of the actions of the same Word, operating at different stages of the history of salvation, and providing exact correspondences because they are indeed the actions of a single Word. We find here once more the principle which arose when we were speaking of types. The realities of which Scripture tells us do not refer to data foreign to Scripture, but to other realities in Scripture. It is this correspondence which, by showing us the perfect unity of this activity of one and the same Word, calls forth within us the proof of its reality. We can reach the Gospel through the Eucharist, Mysticism through the Gospel, the Old Testament through the New. It matters little which approach we take. It is always the same Word performing the works of God in mankind who remains the sole object of faith.

. . . . .

If evil were a problem that depended on man's good-will for its solution, Christ need only have been a preacher, and 'Moral Rearmament' would be the true expression of His will. But Christ came to die, and in this He shows us that evil is a mystery. It is not only the expression of man's ill-will; it is the state of spiritual death in which the whole of mankind is involved as a result of the ill-will of the first man. This state of death affects man both in his soul and in his body. It makes him the prisoner of the prince of this

[1] St. John 6 [50].

world; it separates him from the living God; it is absolute misery, the hopeless position from which man is utterly incapable of freeing himself by his own strength.

It is this that causes the Passion of Christ to be linked with the deepest human experience. It is not only a matter of being moved by the suffering and death of a righteous man. It is not merely a question of the exemplary and quasi-mythical expression of the victory of love over self, nor of a metaphysical mediation which reconciles opposites, nor of the heroic triumph of the spirit over the death of the flesh. It is something more fundamental that the Cross sets out to deal with in the heart of man, the experience of a state of captivity from which there is no escape, the extremity-state of death. Technical progress may free man from some forms of slavery, but this is an abyss which it cannot touch, and which lies at a far greater depth. Only the Word of God can enter there; and that is why all other answers are superficial.

It is in the Passion of Christ that the ultimate secret of man's destiny is at once unveiled and unfolded. Only the invisible Lamb can break the seals that have kept the book of fate closed. He unveils it by revealing the depth of misery, the true nature of sin, the power of the forces of evil. It is in the light of the Cross that man knows what he is. And if it were not for this light He could not bear the accompanying Revelation. But the Passion of Christ unfolds human destiny as well as unveiling it. The Passion only shows us the abyss in order at the same time to show us the Word of God going down into that abyss to confront the forces of evil and break the power which they wielded over captive humanity. Superficial minds may be complacent and try to forget. They construct for themselves a universe in which there is neither sin, passion, nor resurrection. But it is this closed universe that is the very prison in which a disguised Satan keeps his prey captive. And it is this prison whose brazen bars are burst asunder by the Passion of Christ.

Truly the paradox of the God-Man appears in all its splendour in the Passion of Christ. To the onlooker, to the Roman soldier who guards it, what could be more absurd than the wretched body of the Jew hanging on the gibbet, an object from which His friends of yesterday recoil in horror! It is this that will go down in any record that is content with surface impressions. Yet what happens on the Cross is the key event in the history of the world. It is the fulfilment of that mysterious plan which was foreshadowed by the Paschal Lamb and the sacrifice of Isaac—and which perhaps in the millennial depths of time was already foretold by man's first suffering, the consequence of man's first sin and already the first outline of that sin's reparation.[1] And this happening resounds to the farthest ends of the cosmos, in the vastness of the heavens where the sun is darkened, in the abysses of the earth whence the holy patriarchs arise,[2] in the depths of the sanctuary whose veil is rent.

Beyond are the powers of the heavens which are shaken. Satan falls like a flash of lightning. 'Sentence is now being passed on this world; now is the time when the prince of this world is to be cast out.'[3] It is the καιρός, the hour, of which Christ said at Cana that it had not yet come, the hour that is unique in the history of the world, that of the decisive happening—the hour that is unique in the history of all men, that of the ultimate decision. Satan is robbed of the power that man's sin had lent him over the cosmic

---

[1] See Cyril von Korvin Krasinsky, 'La création comme Temple et Royaume de l'Homme-Dieu, *Enkainia*, 1956, pp. 222-224.
[2] Matt. 26 [51-52].   [3] John 12 [31].

sphere, over the noosphere. Robbed of their prey, too, are the bad angels scattered through the air, through the principalities and powers, for the Crucified Word has 'put them to an open shame, led them away in triumph through him.'[1] It is this cosmic struggle that is described in Hippolytus' inspired sermon: 'He grasps from all sides in His mighty hands the manifold spirit of the air.'[2]

The earliest sermons about the Cross celebrate its cosmic character. 'I know thy mystery, O cross, for which thou wast raised up. Indeed thou wast raised up over the world, to make steady that which was unsteady. One part of thee rises into the heavens, to point to the Word on High; another part stretches to right and left, to put to flight the fearsome power of the adversary and to gather the world together in unity; and one part of thee is planted in the earth, so that thou mayest unite the things that are on the earth and the things in hell with the things that are in heaven.'[3] Paul had already written that 'it was God's good pleasure to let all completeness dwell in him, and through him to win back all things, whether on earth or in heaven, into union with himself, making peace with them through his blood, shed on the cross.'[4]

The content of this act of the Word is of inexhaustible richness. It is the victory of the Word over the powers of evil, over the prince of this world; it is the liberation of captive humanity. In this respect it repeats in an infinitely greater fashion the liberation of God's captive people from the ruler of Egypt, who is the symbol of this world. It is the union of 'dead'[5] mankind with the Word, the supreme extension of the Incarnation into human nature

[1] Col. 2 14. So Knox, but our author says 'through the Cross', which Knox in a note accepts as a possible alternative.—Trans.
[2] 51; *Sources Chrétiennes*, 178.
[3] *Martyrdom of Andrew*, 14; Bonnet, 54–55.   [4] Col. 1 19-20.
[5] Gregory of Nyssa, *Discours catéchétique*, XXXII, 3. 'en état de cadavre.'

in all its disintegration, in order to bear the spark of the divine life into the very heart of misery, to destroy evil at the root, and to enable a regenerate humanity to flourish on the ancient stock of Adam. It is the priestly act which obtains perfect glory for God by revealing the sovereign holiness of His divine will through obedience to death, and by covering in this manner a multitude of sins.

This is why, if Christ, God and Man, sums up the entirety of God's plan, the Cross in its turn sums up the entirety of Christ's plan. It reaches the limits of the world of spirits; it resumes possession of man as he was originally and accomplishes his final fulfilment; it reveals the ultimate depths of the Love of the Trinity. 'But here, as if God meant to prove how well he loves us, it was while we were still sinners that Christ . . . died for us.'[1] The Cross sums up the whole teaching of St. Paul: 'What we preach is Christ crucified.'[2] The Cross is signed on the forehead of the child as a protection against the forces of evil. The Cross brings about, in baptism, the regeneration of the catechumen, and amongst the friends of God a mystical transformation. And it is the Cross, the Sign of the Son of Man, that shall appear in the last days upon the clouds of heaven, as a star to herald the rising of the eternal sun.

. . . . .

For many minds, the Resurrection of Christ represents the point at which they stop short. Up to the time of His Passion Christ is a historical figure. From the Resurrection onward, He belongs to the realm of faith. And it is true that the Resurrection is indeed a dividing line. Up to the time of His burial, the life of Christ is unfolded on the level of ordinary human existence. From the time of the Resurrection, He enters a different order, that of transfigured

[1] Rom. 5 8.   [2] I Cor. I 28.

humanity. But it remains true that this contrast is much less important than it appears at first sight. The whole purpose of the pages which have led up to this chapter has been to show that from its outset the life of Christ belonged to the domain of the mighty works of God. Already we were deep in mystery. And if that life was unfolded on the level of ordinary human existence, this does not mean that that existence represented a natural order as opposed to a supernatural world. It was already related to a supernatural world, that of human nature in its state of misery and corruptibility. In that He was made flesh, the Word of God was accessible to carnal man. But this carnal condition is only one of the states of humanity, that of its fall.

When we come to the Resurrection, the opposite is true. The Word of God withdraws His Manhood from the carnal condition, and thus conceals it from the gaze of carnal man. But as it is that same Manhood which exists first of all in the conditions of the flesh, and now exists in the conditions of the spirit, it is clear that this transition is bound to have a 'footprint' in the world of the flesh. This footprint, this symbol, is the empty tomb. It is a negative symbol, which in no way enables us to grasp the essential content of the Resurrection, for that is inaccessible to the flesh, and no historian or philosopher will ever encounter it in the course of applying his own technique. But this negative symbol is highly important, inasmuch as it encompasses the empty space wherein the Resurrection takes place, and sets its very locality within the pattern of ordinary history.

This is the very reason why it undoubtedly constitutes the fact which those who seek to separate the Jesus of history from the Jesus of faith are most often forced to reject. Already the Jews had spread the rumour that the disciples had stolen the body of Christ, which is perhaps the most valuable evidence for the existence of the open tomb. Later the very reality of the fact was to be challenged, or its whole meaning was to be denied. It is more convenient, indeed, to dissociate the two levels entirely from one another, and to protect the Christ of faith by detaching Him completely from the results of historical criticism. But the empty tomb is just what prevents us from placing the heavenly story of the Word side by side with the earthly story of Jesus, and thus compels us to recognize that the Word has really come in the flesh, and that the flesh in its turn is really quickened by the Word. So we are obliged to maintain the rigorous continuity of the Jesus of history with the Jesus of faith, but seeing them simply as two states of the single Manhood of Jesus.

But if it is an integral part of Christ's Manhood, the Resurrection is equally an integral part of the continuity of the works which the Trinity performs in and through the Manhood of Christ. The Resurrection may even be called the supremely divine work, because it is strictly the divinization of man by the virtue of the Spirit. It is not only a reanimation, which would be merely a return to and a prolonging of mortal life, even if that life were to be prolonged indefinitely. But it is the passing from one mode of existence to another. The death from which it frees the Manhood of Christ is not only the separation of soul and body, but the mortal condition as such, of which the separation of soul and body is only the final expression. And the life which it communicates is not the state of man while his soul animates his body; it is the life of God grasping the soul and body, removing them from the misery of the flesh and communicating to them the glory of the Spirit.

It is in the Resurrection that the condition of man as it is present in the eternal design of God is brought to fulfilment.

For God created man for incorruptibility. From the beginning He set man in Paradise, that is, in the midst of divinizing energies. It is sin that reduced man to the condition of the flesh by separating him from the life of God. In Christ once more, and this time for ever, mankind is quickened by the life of the Spirit. This is accomplished first and foremost in the Manhood of Christ, in order that it may be the instrument by which that life may be communicated to the rest of mankind. 'His was the first birth out of death; thus in every way the primacy was to become his.'[1]

. . . . .

With the Resurrection, however, the mysteries of the Christian epoch, properly so called, are not brought to an end, nor are the final conditions presented for the pouring out of the Spirit upon mankind. This humanity, with which He became one, which He washed in His blood, which He caused to appear before Him in immaculate holiness in the brightness of His Resurrection, is now brought into His Father's House on the day of the Ascension to celebrate there an eternal union. The Gospel records that this happens at the end of those mysterious forty days during which the risen Christ appears in the midst of His Apostles to give them His final teaching. And this period of the life of Christ is not the least important in relation to our present subject, on account of the dividing line which it represents between the life of Christ in the flesh and His final entry into the glory of the Father.

The Ascension presents an outward viewpoint, that of the cloud which concealed Jesus from the sight of His disciples while He was being carried up into heaven. The Ascension also has a theological aspect, which makes it

[1] Col. I 18.

one of the great mysteries of the life of Christ. It is not only visibly above the heavens, it is invisibly above every creature that Christ's Manhood is exalted, amid the awe-struck hosts of angelic worlds. It is thus that St. Paul presents it in the Epistle to the Ephesians when he shows us how God by a mighty exercise of power 'raised Christ from the dead, and bade him sit on his right hand above the heavens, high above all princedoms and powers and virtues and dominations, and every name that is known, not in this world only, but in the world to come. He has put everything under His dominion.'[1]

Thus the Ascension appears as the counterpart of the Incarnation. The Word of God came down from His kingly house to seek for the lost sheep, mankind. Now, having found it again, He bears it on His shoulders and lays it in the sheepfold. The Ascension therefore marks the completion of the movement begun at the Incarnation, the climax of the action of the divine *agape* in seeking for man to lead him into the realm of the Trinity. It is also the counterpart of the humiliations of the Cross. The Son had glorified the Father by accepting 'an obedience which brought him to death, death of a cross. That is why God has raised him to such a height, given him that name which is greater than any other name; so that everything in heaven and earth and under the earth must bend the knee before the name of Jesus.'[2]

This is what makes the Ascension the supreme cosmic mystery. Not only does the glorified Christ become the Head of the Church which is His Body, but He becomes the Lord of all creation. It is sometimes asked if spiritual beings who might be discovered upon some unknown nebula would not be strangers to the mystery that was

[1] Eph. 1 20-22.   [2] Phil. 2 8-10.

accomplished on earth, and would not call for other in-
carnations. Paul has already answered this question by
declaring that Christ has been made Lord of everything
that can be named. Moreover, the divine acts performed
on earth in the death, Resurrection and Ascension of Christ
have an absolutely universal value. The earth is not the
cosmological centre of the universe, and it is not certain
that it is the peak of cosmic evolution. But there can be
no doubt that it is the theological centre of the universe,
and the scene of the decisive event. The two are not bound
up with one another. The mistake which Galileo's enemies
made lay in thinking that they were.

On the day of the Ascension the Word of God, sent by
the Father, having been united with human nature and
washed it in the blood of His Passion, leads humanity
like a spotless Bride into His Father's House. On the day of
Pentecost the work of the Spirit begins. Sent by the Father
and the Son, the Spirit causes the new creation, the cosmos
of the Church, to spring into being, as, at the beginning
of the world, He raised up the first creation, the cosmos of
nature, out of the primaeval waters. However, between
the Ascension and Pentecost there is a mysterious pause,
brief by human reckoning, but representing by itself a
whole epoch in which, in a silence like that which precedes
the creation of the world, the dwelling-place of the Spirit
is established by decree in the secrecy of the divine counsels.

These ten days are almost empty of earthly events. The
Apostles have returned to Jerusalem after the Ascension.
They have come together in the Upper Room. And there
'all these, with one mind, gave themselves up to prayer,
together with Mary the mother of Jesus, and the rest of
the women and his brethren.'[1] Only one event is mentioned

---

[1] Acts I [14].

in Acts, the choosing of Matthias, which in view of the approach of Pentecost makes the Apostolic body, which had been mutilated by Judas' betrayal, once more an integral whole. But nothing else happens. The scene is changed from earth to heaven. It is there that the real events of this period occur. They are concealed from human sight, 'utterly mysterious and unknowable,' hidden in the thick cloud which, since the Ascension, has veiled them from the Apostles 'as they strained their eyes towards heaven.'[1]

Does Scripture enable us to catch some glimpse of these events, which are nevertheless among the most important in sacred history? Through the Ascension, the Manhood with which the Word of God is united is brought into the realm of the life of the Trinity, far above all creatures, amid the wonder of the angels. The heavenly liturgy is set in motion around Him. 'Everything in heaven . . . must bend the knee before the name of Jesus.'[2]

But the word of God has brought into the life of the Trinity the Manhood with which He is united, only in order to 'prepare a home'[3] for His brethren. Had He not said 'If only I am lifted up from the earth, I will attract all men to myself'?[4] Installed henceforth in His royal dignity, seated at the right hand of God, 'he now appears in God's sight on our behalf.'[5] He has ascended to the Father only in order to communicate to all His brethren the glory in which His Manhood is arrayed, and in order that He may be made 'the head to which the whole Church is joined, so that the Church is his body, the completion of him who everywhere and in all things is complete.'[6] For He 'has gone up, high above all the heavens, to fill creation with His presence.'[7] It is this outpouring of grace (*dedit dona*

[1] Acts 1 [10]. [2] Phil. 2 [10]. [3] St. John 14 [2-3].
[4] St. John 12 [32]. [5] Heb. 9 [24]. [6] Eph. 1 [22-23].
[7] Eph. 4 [10].

hominibus) which is prepared during these ten days in the bosom of the divine counsels. Henceforth, all is in readiness. The Church is established in her essential structure. The Apostolic body is once more complete. It now remains to bestow life upon it, to quicken it with divine energy. This is the work of the Spirit.

Beyond the Apostles gathered around Mary in the Upper Room, beyond even the awestruck choirs of angels, in a silence like that which preceded the creation of the world, time being, as it were, suspended and the whole universe waiting expectantly, the Son asks the Father to consummate His work upon earth by sending the Spirit, the gift of the Father and of the Son, for He proceeds from the Father and from the Son. This is appropriately the mystery that is accomplished during the ten days between the Ascension and Pentecost, between the glorification of the Son and the sending of the Spirit which is its sequel. It is the mystery which Mary contemplates, with all the powers of her soul united in God. But it is so hidden a mystery that Scripture scarcely permits us a glimpse of it.

Indeed, the mystery of the ten days is left in silence. Between the seating of Christ at the right hand of God and the sending of the Apostles, there is, as it were, a hiatus. 'And so,' writes St. Mark, 'the Lord Jesus, when he had finished speaking to them, was taken up to heaven, and is seated now at the right hand of God; and they went out and preached everywhere.'[1] St. Paul is scarcely more explicit: 'He who went down is no other than he who has gone up, high above the heavens, to fill all creation with his presence. Some he has appointed to be apostles, others to be prophets . . .'[2] Was the mystery of this period destined to be known only to the angels? It is true indeed

[1] St. Mark 16 [19].   [2] Eph. 4 [10-11].

that it is the time when the glory of Christ resounded through the angelic worlds, before reaching the churches on earth, as the creative power first raised them into being.

The Beloved Disciple, with deeper insight into the secrets that are beyond the veil, has confided to us something of their import. And His Gospel enables us to glimpse the mysterious stages that precede the outpouring of the Spirit. 'Appearing in God's sight on our behalf,'[1] the only Son, arrayed in the fullness of His priestly role, begins by asking the Father to send the Spirit: 'I will ask the Father, and he will give you another to befriend you, one who is to dwell continually with you for ever.'[2] The first act of the eternal High Priest, 'having entered once for all into the Holy of holies after winning eternal redemption,[3] is to intercede for the multitude of His brethren.'

The mystery of the Upper Room is therefore in the first place that of the prayer of Christ the eternal Priest. This prayer is profoundly mysterious. 'All authority,' He says, 'in heaven and on earth has been given to me'[4]—to Christ arrayed in royal dignity. But the only Son 'cannot do anything at His own pleasure, He can only do what He sees His Father doing.'[5] Just as in His eternal Sonship the Son belongs entirely to His Father, in the same way in the dwelling-place of the Spirit who proceeds from the Father and the Son, the Son refers everything to the Father. 'The Father will send the Holy Spirit on my account.'[6]

Just as, in turn, the Father, in the eternal generation, bestows Himself utterly upon the Son, so in the sending of the Spirit He bestows the Spirit upon the Son. Here it is no longer St. John, but a hidden passage in the Acts of the Apostles, that enables us to glimpse this second stage in

[1] Heb. 9 24.   [2] St. John 14 16.   [3] Heb. 9.
[4] St. Matt. 28 18.   [5] St. John 5 19.   [6] St. John 14 26.

the mystery of the Upper Room: 'And now, exalted at
God's right hand, He has claimed from His Father His
promise to bestow the Holy Spirit; and He has poured out
that Spirit, as you can see and hear for yourselves.'[1]
Certainly the Son already possesses the Spirit. He is united
with Him in the midst of the Trinitarian relationships. He is
united with Him in His Incarnation, when the Spirit rests
upon Mary. He is united with Him in His ministry, when
the Spirit descends upon Him at His Baptism. Finally, He
is united with Him in the Resurrection, which is the work
of the power of the Spirit.

But here it is a matter of a new gift, which inaugurates
a new era in the economy of salvation. It is inasmuch as the
Son has become the Head of the Church that the Father
bestows the Spirit upon Him, in order that the Son may in
His turn give Him to the Church which is His Body. It is
first of all in the glorified Manhood of Christ that the fullness of the Spirit rests. Indeed the Spirit had first to be
bestowed upon Him in order that He might pour it out
upon the Church. As the Scripture says: 'Fountains of
living water shall flow from his bosom. He was speaking
here of the Spirit, which was to be received by those who
learned to believe in him; the Spirit which had not yet been
given to men, because Jesus had not yet been raised to
glory.'[2]

This outpouring of the Spirit now becomes possible.
And in the secrecy of the divine counsels, the sending of
the Spirit is decreed. It is the last and most solemn of the
events that fill the ten days. The promise that Christ had
made to His own is to be fulfilled: 'When the truth-giving
Spirit, who proceeds from the Father, has come to befriend
you . . . he will bear witness of what I was.'[3] And later: 'He

[1] Acts 2 [33].　　[2] St. John 7 [38-39].　　[3] St. John 15 [26].

who is to befriend you will not come to you unless I go, but if only I make my way there, I will send him to you.'[1] Christ ascended to the Father to ask Him for the Spirit. The Spirit was given to Him. He now decides to send Him forth upon His own.

In the Apocalypse, Saint John shows us these mysteries taking place in the silence of God: 'The Lamb, who dwells where the throne is, will be their shepherd, leading them out to the springs whose water is life.'[2] Soon he sees 'a river, whose waters give life; it flows, clear as crystal, from the throne of God, from the throne of the Lamb . . . mid-way along the city street.'[3] But before we contemplate the stream flowing in the midst of the city, the Spirit poured out in the midst of Jerusalem, the birth of the Church, there is the time of silence when that pouring out is decreed in the divine counsels: 'Then he broke open the seventh seal; and, for about half an hour, there was silence in heaven.'[4]

. . . . .

Thus the mysteries of Christ appear to us as the theological content of the episodes of His earthly life. Lives of Christ often stop short at these episodes, and that is why they leave us unsatisfied. In them, we are in contact with the Manhood of Jesus, but we do not see the Divinity of the Word in action. Now it is certainly true that we should start from the Manhood of Jesus. It is through this that the Word seeks us out on our level. It would be a serious error to misunderstand this, and it would be an equally serious error to stop there. Christ first approaches the Samaritan woman by asking her to drink the water from Jacob's well. This is to make her understand that it is

[1] St. John 16 [7].   [2] Apoc. 7 [17].   [3] Apoc. 22,[1-2].   [4] Apoc. 8 [1].

she who should ask Him for the living water that springs from eternal life. And it is in this way that we are introduced to the supremely real content of the life of the Lord Jesus.

BIBLIOGRAPHY

St. Athanasius, *Contre les païens et sur l'incarnation du Verbe.*

L. Bouyer, *The Paschal Mystery*, London, 1952.

G. Aulen, *Christus Victor*, London, 1931.

P. de Surgy, *Les grandes étapes du mystère du salut*, Paris, 1958.

CHAPTER VI

CHRIST AND THE CHURCH

WHEN we speak of the risen Christ we cannot confine ourselves to the historical fact of the Resurrection. 'Christ, now He has risen from the dead, cannot die any more.'[1] The risen Christ is a living reality. It is this new aspect which we shall now examine. From many points of view it is the most important of all, for it brings us to the essential stage of faith. It is a mistake, when thinking of Christ, not to look back towards the past, not to seek Him in the Gospel, not to give a special character to the period of His life on earth. 'Happy are those,' writes Péguy, 'who saw Him pass by in His own country; happy are those who saw Him pass by on this earth . . . Jerusalem, Jerusalem, thou art more blessed than Rome.'[2] But the answer to this is given by St. Paul: 'Even if we used to think of Christ in a merely human fashion, we do so no longer.'[3] It does not matter whether we met Christ on the roads of Galilee; some of those who did so failed to recognize Him. What is important is that we should believe in Him as the living Lord. Like the Magdalen on Easter morning, we seek for Christ among the dead. 'Why,' the angel asks her, 'are you seeking one who is alive, here among the dead?'[4]

This does not mean that we belittle the Christ of the Gospel. That is the exaggeration into which Bultmann is falling to-day. Despairing of ever being able to recognize the face through the documents, he reaches the point of ignoring the importance of that face. It matters little to him whether the Jesus of history is a creation of the com-

---

[1] Rom. 6 [9].
[2] Charles Péguy, *Le mystère de la charité de Jeanne d'Arc, Oeuvres complètes*, p. 38.
[3] 2 Cor. 5 [16].   [4] St. Luke 24 [5].

munity. The only thing that counts is the actual encounter with Him in the καιρός, the decisive event of conversion. This is to misunderstand the reality and importance of the Manhood of Jesus as the Gospel shows Him to us. Bultmann certainly recognizes that the acts performed in Him at a particular moment in time are the decisive event, of which the actual encounter with Him is only the visible sign. But in that he dissociates this from the content which the Gospel gives it, Bultmann ends by withdrawing Christ at once from both secular and sacred history— that is to say, in the last resort, from all history, so as to make of Him nothing more than a mere event in his own life-story. But having said this, it still remains true that the affirmation of God's present activity in Christ gets down to the root of the matter. All that is necessary now is to see in this an action which is not merely concerned with His existence, but which is recorded in objective history. It is of a piece with the actions of God in the Old Testament. It relates to the central event which is represented by the mysteries of the life of Christ. It is continued objectively in the sacraments of the Church. And to the extent to which I share in this life of the Church so does this action reach out to me in my personal life. The mistake always lies in isolating one of these aspects and belittling the others. Our intention, on the contrary, is to show their strict continuity. And it is in this perspective that the present action of Christ takes place.

The Apostles' Creed contains a noteworthy passage in which, grammatically speaking, we move from the past to the future: 'He ascended into the heavens (*ascendit ad coelos*). He is seated (*sedet*) at the right hand of God. He will come again (*venturus est*) to judge the living and the dead.' Thus the mysteries of Christ are not completed.

with the Ascension. There is still another mystery to come, that of the Parousia. Between these two there is a mystery which is, in the present, that of the session at the right hand. So there is a mystery of Christ with which we are contemporary, which corresponds to that moment of sacred history which belongs to us, which constitutes the present activity of the Word. And this mystery is the one through which the Manhood of the Word, introduced into the sphere of the Trinity by the Ascension, becomes the instrument for the sanctification of all men.

This confronts us with a most important observation. Sacred history does not end with the New Testament. It will only be completed at the time of the Parousia; and it fills the whole intervening period. We live in the midst of sacred history. And if sacred history means the history of the *magnalia Dei*, this means that we are living in a world in which the Word of God is performing, in our midst, divine works which are the equivalent of the great works of God in the Old and New Testaments, and their continuation in the era of the Church. There is such a thing as secular history, which is that of the great works of man. And indeed those works have their greatness. But the works which God performs are infinitely greater. And it is the property of faith to grasp them by means of the prophetic mind which alone can penetrate that mystery. If the works of man bear witness to what man can do, the works of God bear witness to what God can do.

The Christian must understand this hierarchy of order. It will always remain true, according to Pascal, that the greatness of sanctity, that is, divine works properly so called, infinitely surpasses the greatness of bodies and spirits. This does not mean that the latter are not truly great in their respective spheres. As Péguy said, 'it is not

necessary to humiliate Severus to exalt Polyeuctes.'
Christianity has no need, as Marx complains in *The Holy
Family*, to rob man in order to exalt God. On the contrary,
the greater man appears to us, the more we shall understand
how great God is. Yet it will always remain true that the
greatness of sanctity prevails over the greatness of bodies
and spirits. And it will always be scandalous to see
Christians being too much impressed with worldly greatness, whether it be that of politics, science or art.

Thus the era of the Church is simply the present form of
the mighty works of the Trinity and the continuation of the
mystery of the Incarnate Word. Each new undertaking in
the history of salvation enriches it with a new reality
which is perpetuated in the succeeding stages, following the
law of the Covenant which is the irreversible character of
the acts of God. What is gained is gained once for all.
And so it is that mankind moves on from glory to glory.
For 'we know how that sentence of death, engraved in
writing upon stone, was promulgated to men in a dazzling
cloud, so that the people of Israel could not look Moses in
the face, for the brightness of it, although that brightness
soon passed away. How much more dazzling, then, must
be the brightness in which the spiritual law is promulgated
to them!'[1]

Here we find, in the mysteries of glory, the order which
we ascertained in the mysteries of darkness. Through the
Ascension, the Manhood of Christ was exalted above every
creature and introduced by the Word into the inaccessible
sanctuary of the Trinity. But the Manhood of Christ
tends to attract everything else to it. 'If only I am lifted
up from the earth, I will attract all men to myself.'[2] Christ
has only entered the heavenly sanctuary as a forerunner.

[1] 2 Cor. 3 7.   [2] St. John 12 32.

The presence of His Manhood in the sphere of the Trinity is the guarantee of the possibility that is henceforth ours to attain. The impassable gulf is henceforth overcome, the impossible has become possible. In a notable image, the Epistle to the Hebrews shows the Manhood of Christ as cast like an anchor, not into the depths of the sea, but into the far places of heaven, laying the foundation of our hope that we shall in our turn attain to the anchorage beyond the veil.[1]

Thus there is, henceforth, in the heart of mankind an ascensional power which lifts it up and draws it towards the Father, that *pondus amoris* of which Augustine spoke, and which counteracts the 'gravity' of the flesh. This is the meaning of the era of the Church, in which Christ, having entered into the glory of the Father, seeks to lift up mankind as a whole. By this means the movement is completed which began at the Incarnation, when the Word of God came to seek for mankind, but in order to lead it back to the Father. 'This is why we are told, He has mounted up on high; he has captured his spoil; he has brought gifts to men. And he who so went down is no other than he who has gone up, high above all the heavens to fill creation with his presence.'[2] And truly this humanity is a mighty weight to raise. Its gravity resists grace. That is the whole drama of the present period in sacred history. But the power of the Word is greater than the resistance of men.

Received into the heavenly sanctuary, the Manhood of Christ has been transfigured by the life of the Spirit in its soul and its body. It has been invested with glory. This communication of the Holy Spirit fills the Manhood of Christ with the fullness of the divine life. But the gift of

---

[1] Heb. 6 [19].   [2] Eph. 4 [8-10].

the Spirit was accepted by Christ so that He might pour it forth at the time of Pentecost.[1] Thus the Manhood of Christ is raised above every creature so as to be henceforth the spring from which eternal life would gush forth upon the world. 'He showed me a river, whose waters give life; it flows, clear as a crystal, from the throne of the Lamb ... mid-way along the city street.'[2]

So on the day of Pentecost, which inaugurates an economy co-extensive with the era of the Church, the glorified Christ pours out upon the Apostles the Spirit which has been given to Him. But He only pours out that Spirit upon men because He was first given to His Manhood. The mystery first takes place in Him, so that it may afterwards take place in us. But it only takes place in Him in order to take place afterwards in us. The glorious Manhood of Christ is thus established for ever in its pre-eminent function. It is the sun illuminating and giving life to the new creation, about which St. John tells us that 'there will be no more need of light from lamp or sun; the Lord God will shed his light on them.'[3] No grace will ever be more than a sharing in His grace; no light will ever be more than a ray of His own effulgent brightness.

This flowing into human nature of the grace first contained in the Manhood of Christ, as at its source, is expressed in Scripture through a series of images, each of which throws one aspect into relief. The first is that of a spring from which the Spirit flows as a fountain of living water bearing all before it, as a river giving rise to life wherever it spreads forth its waves, the cosmic Jordan whose source is in heaven, and which carries up to heaven the souls baptized in its waters. This is the fulfilment of the ancient prophecy. Ezechiel had proclaimed that in the days of

---

[1] Acts 2 ³⁸.   [2] Apoc. 22 ¹⁻².   [3] Apoc. 22 ⁵.

the Messiah a stream of water would flow eastwards from beneath the temple and fall into the eastern sea, the Dead Sea, so as to make all things live.[1] This living water flowed indeed from the pierced side of Christ, the Temple of the New Covenant, to give life not to the fishes of the sea, but to those living souls which should be caught by the fishers of men, and of which the fishes were a type. Thus from the Manhood of Christ, transfigured by the divine energy, the divine life, the Spirit begins to be poured out upon the whole of mankind, so as to give life to all flesh by virtue of the continuity that unites His humanity with the rest of humanity.

Another image is that of fire. The fire of the Spirit—for the Spirit was poured out upon the Apostles as tongues of flame—which had 'caught on' in the Manhood of Christ, begins to spread throughout mankind like a heath-fire. This is no longer the image of the cosmic river, it is that of the cosmic fire which seeks to burn up everything: 'It is fire that I have come to spread over the earth, and what better wish can I have than that it should be kindled?'[2] Perhaps no image could better express what the Church really is, that virtue of the Spirit which works in the depths of humanity, seeking to consume all hardness, to purify all dross, to penetrate all flesh with its incandescence. And certainly the briar-roots are often tough and unwilling. The fire of Purgatory, which is still the fire of the Spirit, must complete the burning of all that remains carnal. For only that which has been transformed into the Son by the devouring flame of the Spirit shall enter into the Father's House.

This life-giving work which spreads from Christ's Humanity upon our own humanities is expressed in still further images in the New Testament. For St. Matthew,

[1] Ezech. 47 [1-9].   [1] St. Luke 12 [49].

it is a leaven which permeates the dough till it is completely leavened, and it is after this parable that Christ adds: 'I will speak my mind in parables, I will give utterance to things which have been kept secret from the beginning of the world.'[1] For St. John, Christ is the vine of which we are the branches: 'If a man lives on in me, and I in him, then he will yield abundant fruit.'[2] The Spirit is here the life-giving sap which alone can bear the fruits of grace. The old vine, the people of Israel, had disappointed God's expectation. Now a new vine is planted which shall bear fruits of life in all those who are grafted into it by baptism. And this vine is the glorious Manhood of Christ which gives rise to the life of the Spirit in the dead branches.

This, too, is the cosmic vine, the cosmic tree whose leaves are lost in the stars, in the angelic worlds, whose deep roots penetrate the abyss to take hold of all its foundations, whose branches stretch out to the farthest bounds of the universe. The ancient Greeks saw in the vine a symbol of immortality, because of the ecstasy of wine which releases man from earthly cares. And the first Christians used this pattern in the paintings in the catacombs. But it denoted the true vine, which is no mere symbol of the soul freed from the cares of the body, but which truly accomplishes the union of soul and body, and releases them from mortality by immersing them in the life of the Spirit.

A final comparison is that of St. Paul; and the text is all the more remarkable for being directly connected with the mystery of the Ascension and of the entry of Christ into His royal state: 'He who so went down is no other than he who has gone up, high above all the heavens, to fill creation with his presence. Some he has appointed to be

---

[1] St. Matt. 13 33-35.   [2] St. John 15 5.

apostles, others to be prophets, others to be evangelists, or pastors, or teachers. They are to . . . build up the frame of Christ's body, until we all realize our common unity through faith in the Son of God, and fuller knowledge of him. So we shall reach perfect manhood, that maturity which is proportioned to the completed growth of Christ; we are no longer to be children. We are to follow the truth, in a spirit of charity, and so grow up, in everything, into a due proportion with Christ, who is our head.'[1] Christ exalted to the glory of the Father is here the head, the chief. And it is inasmuch as the Body which is the Church is continually linked with Him that it is built up little by little until it reaches its full stature.

A stronger indication could hardly be given of the continuity of the glorious Manhood of Christ with the 'pilgrim' Church, the complementary character shared by Christ's Manhood and the Church, which is its fullness. And so the work of the Trinity in the present time is the building up of the Body of Christ. This work is the continuation of what the Trinity first substantially performed in the Manhood of Christ, and it is brought to fruition through the sacrament of this glorified Manhood. This represents a single plan, the whole Christ, of whom Augustine wrote, the Head and the Body. This work is the work of the Word sent by the Father and acting through the Spirit who was first at work in Him, in His Manhood, and then through Him, through this Manhood, in the Church, the new creation of the universe of grace. So, as Gregory of Nyssa says, Christ Himself builds up His own Body.[2]

. . . . .

We have not yet spoken of all the characteristics of the

[1] Eph. 4 10-15.   [2] *P.G.*, XLIV, 1317 C.

activity of the glorified Christ in the era that is ours. We must also add that this activity occurs through the intermediary of the Church; it implies a special relationship between Christ and the Church. Here again we have a remarkable feature. The Trinity could act directly on individual souls, but the economy which He has chosen — is a different one. It is within and through a community that He operates. The sacraments, which are the instruments of this present action of the Word, therefore assume by this means a new significance. They become the expression of the fact that it is through contact with the Church that Christ's grace is given. They appear as communal acts. It is certainly Christ who acts in them and through them. They signify that this action of Christ is brought about through the intermediary of the Church. They presuppose, therefore, a very special relationship between Christ and the Church. It is this relationship which we have now to define.

We have already encountered it on the level of Christ's public life. We asserted that the establishment of the Church's structure was the essential task of this part of the life of Christ. This is clearly one of the aspects in which the continuity of the Christ of history and the Christ of faith is most apparent. The Church, present in our midst, visibly continues the institution whose visible foundation was laid by Christ during His earthly life. She is therefore the most obvious visible link with the Jesus of history. But at the same time the Church invisibly contains the divine acts of Christ in His Passion and Resurrection. She is not only a visible institution; she is the setting of the *magnalia Dei* in our midst. She belongs to the world of mystery.

The Church is the visible organ which the invisible Christ

uses to distribute His invisible gifts to visible men. She depends essentially on the distribution to all mankind of the grace contained in the glorious Manhood of Christ. She possesses no other treasure but this. But this is the special treasure which she alone possesses. She is the point in the world at which the divinizing energies are at work, not in a spatial enclosure like the Temple at Jerusalem, but in a spiritual Temple made of living stones. It is in her that the risen Christ is present to perform His wondrous works. That is why it is towards her alone that whoever seeks to find the risen Christ must turn. She is the meeting-place of the risen Christ and the human soul. And the sacraments are that meeting.

Thus the Church does not possess anything which is properly her own. When she infallibly defines a dogma by the authority of the Sovereign Pontiff, it is not in the name of human authority. It would be blasphemous pride to claim for a man the possession of absolute truth. When she distributes the holy and sanctifying sacraments, it is not the holiness of the distributor that she bestows on others. For he may himself be a sinner. Thus she represents no authority but that of Christ, no sanctity but that of Christ, no truth but that of Christ. Yet she distributes a sanctity, she bears witness to a truth, she exercises an authority, all of which are strictly divine, because they are the very sanctity, authority, and truth of Christ acting in her and through her.

This authority, sanctity, and truth are really possessed by the Church in a manner that is inalienable, incorruptible, and indefectible. And this is so because Christ, who is her Bridegroom, gave them to her once for all and never withdraws His gifts. This is the very mystery of the Covenant. Already in the Old Testament the Covenant signifies the gift by God of a divine reality, an irrevocable gift which cannot be abolished by the faithlessness of the recipient, an exclusive gift which is made to no one else. We find ourselves once more in the region of those divine ways which reappear throughout the centuries of sacred history, and with which the latter makes us gradually familiar. No man has power over God and the things of God, but God has given the Church power over His gifts by an entirely free gift, so that she may infallibly distribute them to the world.

We are confronted with purely divine works performed in our midst. We said that we lived in the fullness of sacred history, and that sacred history was that of the works of God. Similarly the infallibility of the Church is a strictly divine work which God performs in men who of themselves and by their own judgement are subject to error. It was thus with the Old Covenant. How could the New Covenant fail to provide us with a similar truth? In the Old Covenant infallibility was given to the Prophets for the purpose of heralding Christ's coming. In the Church it is given for the purpose of preserving unaltered the deposit transmitted by Christ who has already come, and who upholds His own until the consummation of the world.

So it is with the sacraments. The power to forgive sins is purely divine. The Pharisees are right: 'Who can forgive sins but God alone?' No human authority has the right to assume this power. But Christ gave this power to the Church. It is bound up with her in such a way that, when the priest pronounces the sacramental words, sins are actually forgiven. Thus God is not bound by man, but has freely consented to bind Himself to man, so that He actually gives man power over things that do not belong to him, like the steward who looks after his master's goods although they are not his own, but who has, so to speak, power of attorney over them inasmuch as he is legally entrusted with their care.

It so happens that there are critics who object that these claims weaken to some extent the unique causality of Christ's glorious Manhood. This would be true if we were claiming that the Church maintains anything on her own account. But she has nothing that is not given. Only the gift that she has received is not simply that of holiness, but that of making holy. This appears as a pre-eminent work of the Word. The Church is, in this sense, a wondrous creation. We find in her all the features that belong to the ways of God. And so it is that, far from the supreme dignity that we recognize in the Church preventing us from giving God alone the glory which is His due, it actually causes us to glorify Him all the more because the works which He performs in her are wondrous works. For just as, when in Mary we hail the Immaculate Mother of the Incarnate Word, we do not exalt a woman above the human condition, but magnify God who wrought great things in her, so, when we hail in the Church the immaculate Bride of the Incarnate Word, we do not exalt a human society above the condition of human societies, but glorify God who has given to the Church His Bride, as a specific dowry, all the good things that are His.

This enables us to place the order of the Church in its proper perspective in the *magnalia Dei*, in the history of salvation. We may say that these works of God are performed in two ways which are, moreover, closely connected with one another. On the one hand, there is the action of the Word in souls. The events of sacred history in the present time are, in this perspective, the works which the Word performs in the hidden world of human hearts:

conversion, sanctification, vocation, all the illuminations, graces, charismata, that comprise the vast domain of holiness, the whole order of charity in Pascal's sense of the word. These are the divine works which proceed from the action of the Word and the Spirit, and which arouse, enlarge, and consummate the spiritual life, that is to say, the life which the Spirit brings about in human hearts.

Besides this there are those public, objective works which are the acts of the Church, and which are divine works. They are works of the Church as such, in other words they are something other than the strictly sanctifying acts of the Word in souls. They are the acts that represent the means by which these sanctifying acts are to be accomplished. They constitute that order which is frequently misunderstood by Protestants, who tend only to recognize as divine acts those which God performs in individuals, and to regard the public aspects of Christendom as human institutions. That is why it would seem that for them there is nothing more that can be properly spoken of as living sacred history. But this is to mutilate the works of the Word, to leave on one side an essential aspect of the history of salvation.

These two aspects obviously cannot be separated from one another, but are interdependent. The spiritual life cannot blossom except in a sacramental setting, which is the new Paradise, suffused with streams of grace, in which the new Adam develops. It is the property of Christian sanctity to be the unfolding in us of the life of the risen Christ. Now the risen Christ is present in the Church, and it is through the Church that He is given to us. This is what sharply distinguishes Christian sanctity from all ordinary self-discipline, whatever incidental similarities there may be in methods or practices. It is this sacramental basis of holiness which is misconstrued by all those who only emphasize inward experience and who fail to recognize the mediation of the Church.

Inversely, the sacramental life is wholly directed towards holiness. It is not an end in itself. It represents one side of the Church, her institutional aspect, which is inseparable from her other side, her personal aspect. It is this latter aspect which we described in our previous section when speaking of the doctrine of the Body of Christ or the cosmic Vine. And the Church is just that—the community of saints. But the Church is also an institution; in other words, she is that by which the community of saints is established. She is that which establishes and is established. She is the instrument of the Trinity by which the Word is proclaimed, and she is the community of those who hear the Word. She is the end and object of the work of God, the fullness of Christ, and she is the means whereby that end is attained. She is at once what the Word performs in her and what He performs through her. In this she shares the state of her Spouse the Incarnate Word, who is at once the end and the means of the work of God.

It is essential to remember that the institution is God's work, quite as much as the event. And it is for this reason that the Church as an institution is an essential aspect of sacred history. For the Church is precisely the institution itself, inasmuch as it expresses an irrevocable commitment, which is the characteristic feature of the God of the Covenant. Now the Church is precisely the expression of an irrevocable gift of divine life which the Trinity has actually made to mankind by Jesus Christ. That life is actually possessed by the Church, however unfaithful this or that member may be. She is primarily holy inasmuch as she makes holy, inasmuch as she is qualified to distribute, although she is composed of men, blessings which are properly divine. It is in this way that she is the Bride of Christ, who has given her all He possesses, as an irrevocable and exclusive dowry. This is a wondrous work, in keeping with the ways of the Covenant, its supreme expression.

·   ·   ·   ·   ·

The mission of the Church is carried out in a world that is always stained with sin, a fact which fits in with one of her essential characteristics, namely that she is always encountering opposition. We shall notice the conspicuous place in Christ's teaching of His disciples which is occupied by the foretelling of the persecutions that they are to suffer. This already appears in the Synoptic Gospels: 'I am sending prophets and wise men and men of learning to preach to you; some of them you will put to death and crucify, some you will scourge in your synagogues, and persecute them from city to city.'[1] The last discourse of Jesus in St. John's Gospel is full of these predictions: 'I have told you this, so that your faith may not be taken unawares. They will forbid you the synagogue; nay, the time is coming when anyone who puts you to death will claim that he is performing an act of worship to God.'[2]

The struggle takes place in ordinary history. The persecution that the Church has suffered from the beginning is one of the aspects under which she is revealed in secular history, precisely because this aspect expresses her encounter with world history in earthly cities. The earliest non-Christian evidences which we have about the Church, those of Pliny the Younger, Tacitus, or Suetonius, are concerned with the persecutions of the Church under Nero or with the problems she presented to Roman officials under Trajan. This also expresses the mystery of the

[1] St. Matt. 23 ³⁴.   [2] St. John 16 ¹⁻².

Church. It is this aspect that St. John puts forward in his Apocalypse when describing the same events as those reported by Roman historians, but seeing them from the standpoint of the history of salvation, that is, as an expression of the battle between Christ and the Prince of this world, continuing in the time of the Church.

It is under the form of a conflict in which Christ and the Church are opposed by the forces of evil, whose instrument is the pagan peoples, that the Apocalypse presents the persecutions. Chapter 19 shows us the battles of the Word: 'I saw a white horse appear. Its rider bore for his title, the Faithful, the True; he judges and goes to battle in the cause of right. . . . The name by which he is called is the Word of God; the armies of heaven followed him, mounted on white horses and clad in linen, white and clean. . . . And then I saw the beast and the kings of the earth muster their armies, to join battle with the rider on the white horse and the army which followed him.'[1] Thus for St. John the time of the Church is very much the con--tinuation of the works of the Word of God, for the Word is both the power to arouse faith through the word of the Apostles, and also the process of Revelation; it is the power to arouse the divine life, and also the work of creation and sanctification. Over and above this, it is 'a sharp sword' which carries out judgement by bringing men to know themselves at its prompting.

The battle is at the same time that of the Church and of the power of evil, because, as we have said, the Church shares the whole destiny of the Incarnate Word in His present history. This is the battle that St. John describes in his twelfth chapter, when he contrasts 'a woman that wore the sun for her mantle, with the moon under her

[1] Apoc. 19 [11-19].

feet, and a crown of twelve stars about her head' with 'a
great dragon . . . with seven heads and ten horns, and on
each of the seven heads a royal diadem.'[1] The Church
appears in her transcendent reality, already exalted with
Christ her Bridegroom beyond every creature, and identical
at the same time with God's people, who are symbolized
by the twelve stars. And at the same time the reality of
the persecuting powers of the earth, the seven diadems
and the ten horns, appears in the form of the dragon, the
'serpent of the primal age . . . he whom we call the devil,
or Satan.'[2] Thus the drama of the visible Church assumes
cosmic dimensions as the expression of the fight between
the transcendent Church and the demonic powers.

This fight appears first of all as the continuation of a
fundamental aspect of sacred history. Right at the beginning of that history, the woman was confronted by the
primal serpent. And it is clear that St. John is thinking of
the first Eve when he describes the woman crowned with
stars, triumphing over the serpent whose victim the first
Eve had been. The entire Old Testament had borne
witness to a struggle between the forces of evil, worshipped
as gods by other nations, and the people of Israel, worship-
ping the true God. Christ, in the scene of the Temptation,
is confronted with the Prince of this world, who offers Him
all the kingdoms of the earth, whose master he thus claims
to be. Christ, throughout His life, drives out demons.
Finally, in His Passion, He faces the Prince of this world in
his domain and triumphs over him for ever, destroying
the power which he holds over captive humanity.

The struggle of the Church against the powers of evil
is a sequel to Christ's struggle, but represents in this struggle
a period which is proper to the Church. By the Resurrection

---

[1] Apoc. 12 ¹⁻³.   [2] Apoc. 12 ⁹.

of Christ, indeed, the power of evil has been uprooted. Those who are in Christ are henceforth no longer in its power. On the one hand the Prince of this world still retains his power over those who are not in Christ, who reject Him and thus dissociate themselves from His victory; and, on the other hand, if the Prince of this world no longer has any power over the souls of those who are in Christ, he can still persist in attacking them, both through temptation and persecution, by seeking to lead them inwardly astray through the passions, or to defeat them outwardly by destruction. Henceforth the final issue is no longer in doubt. The power of Satan is no more than a reprieve for him. But that reprieve represents one of the aspects of the time of the Church.

This period is at once a time of grace and a time of ungodliness. The Apocalypse symbolizes this in a remarkable passage: 'Then I was given a reed, shaped like a wand, and word came to me, Up, and measure God's temple, and the altar, and reckon up those who worship in it. But leave out of thy reckoning the court which is outside the temple; do not measure it, because it has been made over to the Gentiles, who will tread the holy city under foot for the space of forty-two months.'[1] It is not a question here of any actual division, but of two aspects of the Church. The outer court is her external, visible reality; under this aspect she is delivered over to the nations, trampled under foot, persecuted. This is the region over which Satan may have power through his earthly tools. On the other hand, the sanctuary represents the inward, invisible reality of the Church; she is already raised up into the mystery of God. And this region, the sanctuary of baptized souls, is inaccessible to the forces of evil. It is

[1] Apoc. 11 1-2.

the same Church that is both delivered over to the nations in her body, and hidden in God in her soul.

This contrast represents an essential distinction in the time of the Church. On the one hand it occurs after the Resurrection, that is, after the decisive event. The victory of Christ is already won; and not only is it won in Christ and for His Manhood, so that the glorification of the latter guarantees the eschatological glorification of the manhood of other men, but—and this is a point on which Catholicism insists—the victory won in Christ is already effective in the souls of those who are united with Him, so that they already live with the life of God, and, in so far as they are faithful to Him, are placed beyond the reach of sin and spiritual death. What is expected is only that that which has already reached their souls should also reach their bodies. 'Beloved, we are sons of God even now, and what we shall be hereafter has not been made known as yet.'[1]

The struggle between Christ and the forces of evil in the time of the Church reaches its fullest expression in the witness of the martyrs. Here again it is to the Apocalypse that we must refer. The martyrs have a prominent place in that book, but the deeper meaning of their struggle is symbolized especially by the theme of the two witnesses in Chapter 11. These latter are the servants of Christ, that is, those who bear witness to His work by word and example, but they cannot testify to the ways of God, that is, finally and in its only true meaning to the destiny of man, without thus condemning the ways of man. Here are two standpoints which are mutually exclusive. This is why 'all who dwell on earth' try to suppress the two witnesses whose presence is a perpetual reproach to them. This reaches its supreme expression in the martyr,

---

[1] 1 St. John 3 [2].

that is, in one who is officially condemned by a lawfully constituted court for the Gospel's sake, and who therefore appears as a claimant to the sovereign rights of the kingdom of heaven over the kingdoms of earth.

But the martyr is not only a witness to the mighty works of God by his confession, he also bears witness by the martyrdom itself. What gives it value, in fact, is not that it expresses heroic courage; if this were so, it would testify simply to man's capacity, not to the value of the cause he serves, for there are men who give their lives for the worst causes. Martyrdom is evidence because he who submits to it is himself a person without courage or heroism, who can only face death because he puts his trust in a divine power which will sustain him. This is the famous saying of Perpetua: 'At that moment, Another will suffer within me.' It is thus that martyrdom is a testimony borne to the divine power (δύναμις) and it appears among the *mirabilia* performed by the Word of God in the time of the Church.

. . . . .

The time of the Church appears also as the period of sacred history in which Christ, the Word of God made flesh, seated at the right hand of the Father, builds up His mystical Body. It is composed of those acts of God which we have been studying under several of their aspects. It remains to be said that the action of the Word in the Church is not the last of the mysteries. After the Seating at the Right Hand, which corresponds to the time of the Church, one mystery is still expected, that of the Return of Christ, the Parousia, which is to be accompanied by the Judgement and the Resurrection. This presents afresh the problem of the meaning of eschatology in Christianity. We have seen that this was one of the essential aspects of the Old Testament, since the latter was a prophecy of eschatological events. We have seen, too, that in Christ the events of faith took place, and eschatology was realized. There can be no doubt that this is the essential feature of Christian eschatology.

It remains true, nevertheless, that if the eschatological events took place in Christ, these events are unfolded in a series of divine acts which, taken together, constitute the events of the End. Among these events, the last has yet to take place, the one that is to round off the work of Christ. This event is indeed the last that is awaited. That is why it seemed to the first Christians to be imminent, as is proved by many passages. It is always characterized by imminence, in that it is always characterized by an immediate spiritual proximity, since no new stage separates us from it, and since we live in the period that immediately precedes it. But this period proves in fact to be longer than the first Christians supposed. And the delay which it represents seems to be connected with the possibility of the Gospel's reaching the whole of mankind and thus giving all men the possibility of salvation.

The content of this final act which brings God's plan to its fulfilment is expressed by St. Paul on two occasions by the term 'manifestation' (ἐπιφάνεια). Thus in the Epistle to the Romans we read: 'If creation is full of expectancy, that is because it is waiting for the sons of God to be made known.'[1] Or again: 'You have undergone death, and your life is hidden away now with Christ in God. Christ is your life, and when he is made manifest, you too will be made manifest in glory with him.'[2] The term 'making manifest' conveys a reality that already existed, but only in a hidden form. It well expresses the content of this mystery.

[1] Rom. 8 [19].   [2] Col. 3 [3-4].

175

Already the work of God was fulfilled in souls: 'You are the sons of God.' But what is expected is the repercussion, upon bodies themselves, upon the material world, upon the cosmos, of the Resurrection of Christ, which thus reaches the utmost ends of creation. For God the Redeemer is also God the Creator. He wishes to lose no part of the creation that is His. He is God the husbandman who comes to gather up the last fragments, to gather a full harvest into His eternal granaries.

These manifestations are first concerned with the Person of Christ. In this sense it is called the Parousia, the Coming. It is the manifestation by Christ of glory upon earth. It is this that is described in the Gospel according to St. Matthew: 'And then the sign of the Son of Man will be seen in heaven; then it is that all the tribes of the land will mourn, and they will see the Son of Man coming upon the clouds of heaven, with great power and glory.'[1] This expectation of Christ's return is profoundly characteristic of Christianity. No more than His first coming, can it be reduced to the simple formula of an encounter with God involving a complete break with the life of the world. It is not merely a fact of consciousness. It springs from the cosmic character of Christianity, which is an interpretation of the totality of history. As such it represents an event which objectively concerns the destiny of the universe and mankind.

This expectation also constitutes the Christian attitude towards existence. It defines the present time of the Church as a tension between what has taken place and what is still to take place. It corresponds to the experience of an existence which is both set free and sanctified, and which nevertheless remains true despite the scandal of suffering

[1] St. Matt. 24 30.

and evil. This twofold aspect appears in the structure of the sacraments. The Eucharist is a memorial of the past mysteries of Christ, it is the sacrament of His real Presence, but it also foretells His Coming, according to Christ's words: 'Do this for a commemoration of me.'[1] This expectation is hope, that is to say, it is the certainty that the promised works will be accomplished. It is patience, the capacity to endure through the time that separates us from an irrevocable fulfilment. It enables the Church to bear persecution in her body, knowing that the hour of deliverance will certainly come.

The Coming of Christ will have for its purpose certain divine works, no less mighty than those which have already been performed, but more glorious. These works take their place in the sequence of God's works at the various stages of sacred history. This Coming is their supreme expression. The first of these works is Judgement. Judgement is the work by which Righteousness, which is God's faithfulness to Himself, performs its work. This Righteousness is entirely positive; it is the fulfilment of the promises made by God. And Judgement is that fulfilment. It is manifestation, in other words, it brings to an end the order of present things, in which true values are hidden and false values are apparent. Judgement exposes the nothingness of that which is not founded upon God, and it necessarily condemns that which is not founded upon God. And it reveals, on the other hand, that what is truly founded upon God has been established for ever. It is the manifestation of the truth. And it manifests the fact that the truth is Christ. It bears witness, then, that those who have believed in Christ have lived in the truth. Thus 'it will be for him to prove the world wrong, about sin, and about rightness

---

[1] ('*Faites ceci, jusqu'à mon retour.*') St. Luke 22 [19].

of heart; I am going back to my Father. . . . About judging; he who rules in this world has had sentence passed on him already.'[1]

― The second divine work is Gathering. 'The Son of Man . . . will send out his angels with a loud blast of the trumpet, to gather his elect from the four winds, from one end of heaven to the other.'[2] This Gathering was, in the Old Testament, one of the essential promises made by God through the Prophets to the scattered people. Christ had already gathered together in Himself not only the scattered people, but the divisions of mankind, and had made of them a single Church. The ancient Liturgy described the day of the final Gathering of those who were thus united but remained separate: 'Gather, O Lord, thy Church, from the towns and cities and markets, from the four corners of the universe.'[3] This is to be the fulfilment of the priestly prayer 'that they should all be one, as we are one.'[4] For unity is a divine work. It is the mark of the life of the Trinity. And the unity of the Church is her visible Epiphany.

― Finally there is Resurrection, the repercussion through bodies and the whole cosmos of that which was already accomplished in the Person of Christ. Resurrection is not merely the bringing back to life of bodies for the purpose of judgement, the general resurrection of the just and the unjust. It is the divine act that bestows incorruptibility upon the bodies of the saints and delivers them from the slavery of spiritual death. Thus the action of God reaches out to the utmost bounds of His creation. For God the Redeemer is also God the Creator. He wishes to lose nothing of the creation that is His. Thus, too, the cosmic

[1] St. John 16 8-11.   [2] St. Matt. 24 30-31.
[3] *Didache* 10 3.   [4] St. John 17 22.

meaning of the Parousia is revealed in its entirety. Beyond humanity it reaches out to the whole cosmos and raises up the new heaven and the new earth.

. . . . .

These chapters dealing with the Mysteries are in fact a commentary on the Christological part of the Apostles' Creed. They show the unity of the action of the Word through the various states in which He is revealed in His life on earth, in His life in the Church, in His glorious Parousia. Some, like the Muslims, retain only the Prophet of Galilee; others, like the Jews, await the eschatological coming of the Messiah. We believe that such views are incomplete and only contain part of the truth. For it is true that Jesus lived on earth; it is true that He shall appear in the clouds of heaven; but it is also true that He is present in the Church. And it is the same Word of God, made one with man's flesh, who is at once 'He who is, and ever was, and is still to come,'[1] and whom the angels hail in all His Parousias as 'He that cometh in the name of the Lord.'[2]

BIBLIOGRAPHY

F. X. Durwell, *La résurrection mystère du salut*, Paris, 1955.

H. Clérissac, *Le mystère de l'église*, Paris, 1925.

E. Mersch, *The Theology of the Mystical Body*, London, 1955.

Ch. Journet, *Théologie de l'église*, Paris, 1957.

Pius XII, *Encyclical Mystici corporis Christi*, 1943.

J. Daniélou, *The Lord of History*, London, 1958.

[1] Apoc. 1 4.   [2] St. Matt. 21 9.

CHAPTER VII

WORD, SACRAMENTS, MISSION

WE have shown in previous chapters the continuity which existed between the different stages in the history of Christ—stages which all spring from the same mystery, at once divine and human, whether it concerns life on earth, the life of the Church, or the eschatological Coming. We must now discuss in more precise terms the mystery of the life of the Church, in order to show how it is placed in continuity with the great works of God in the Old and the New Testaments. These actions of the Word have different forms in the Church, but their focal point is in the sacramental life, which constitutes the new Paradise where the divine energies are at work to sustain the new Adam.

This continuity of the sacraments with the great works of God in the Old and the New Testaments appears in St. John's Gospel, where around the central plan constituted by the life of Jesus another background plan unfolds—the events of the Exodus—and a foreground, which is that of the sacraments. We have here an outstanding example of that correspondence between successive plans of sacred history which constitutes Biblical symbolism and which is the key of David to make known to the mind the design of God. Before speaking of the sacraments, we will begin at once with the Word.

. . . . .

Preaching is not a discourse on God, it is the word of God. It is an act of God working through the ministry of the priest. The word of God for the Bible is not the mere enunciation of a thought. It contains a δύναμις, an efficacy: 'God's word to us is something alive, full of energy;

it can penetrate deeper than any two-edged sword.'[1] It penetrates like a blade right to the heart. 'So it is with the word by these lips of mine once uttered; it will not come back, an empty echo, the way it went; all my will it carries out, speeds on its errand.'[2] It touches hearts and converts them, it arouses faith,[3] it brings about sanctification.[4] It is alive. Nothing can imprison it.

It would be well to write a history of the word of God. It was addressed to Abraham, to Moses. In the time of Samuel, the word of God was rare.[5] Thus the infant Samuel does not recognize it at first and thinks it is Heli who is speaking to him. It is addressed to the Prophets. It upholds them. It was given to them to transmit. It speaks through them. But in Jesus it is the Word Itself which is incarnate, which begins to 'ride' through the world: 'Then, in my vision, heaven opened, and I saw a white horse appear. Its rider bore for his title, the Faithful, the True. . . . The name by which he is called is the Word of God. . . . From his mouth came a two-edged sword.'[6] The word of Christ is a sovereign remedy to convert all hearts. But it also accomplishes works of power. It heals the sick, raises the dead, forgives sins. Power in works and words is one.

This history of the word continues in the Church. The Apostles are its depositories. Their office is the ministry of the word, διακονία τοῦ λόγου.[7] They are the servants of the word. They must preserve it intact.[8] They are ambassadors through whom God speaks.[9] Woe to them if they preach not the Gospel! They hold the Word captive. It is present in its full force, but it must pass through them. They must not let themselves be affected by apparent difficulties. It is not their eloquence which converts. They must have

[1] Heb. 4 [12]. [2] Isa. 55 [11]. [3] 1 Cor. 2 [4].
[4] 1 Tim. 4 [5]. [5] 1 Sam. 3 [1] (i.e. 1 Kings 3 [1]). [6] Apoc. 19 [11-15].
[7] Acts 6 [5]. [8] 2 Cor. 2 [17]. [9] 2 Cor. 5 [20].

confidence in the power of the word. The words which come from their lips reach only the ears of the people, but it is the Word of God which reaches the heart.

This leads us to a new aspect of the question. The Word is the word of God. But this word is expressed through a human organ, and this organ is the Church. The Church is officially sent by the Trinity to proclaim the Gospel to the world. This means that she alone is charged with this office, and that the word is therefore only present in her. We may express the same idea by saying that the Church is the place where the Word of God is present and active. Just as in the Old Testament the people of God alone received and guarded the word, and especially as the Word was in relation to the Shekinah, the indwelling of God in the Temple, so in the New Covenant Christ replaces the Old Temple, and it is in Him that the Word abides. But Christ is the total Christ, the head and the members. And so the Church is the place where the Word of God is heard.

This signifies that henceforth the teaching of the Church is not human teaching. She is merely an intermediary between God and men. It also signifies that this Word was really given by God to the Church, that she is thus infallible as an institution. This is an important matter to take note of against the position of Barth, for whom the word of God is manifested in local communities without ever being tied to an institution. Thus when men ask: 'Has God spoken? Where can we hear God speak?' we can only answer: 'God speaks in the Catholic Church.'

This is of great importance in the theology of preaching. In fact the Church alone is charged with preaching and has authority to do so. Preaching is therefore pre-eminently the official teaching of the Church, expressed through its authorized institutions. It is not private enterprise. It is not personal teaching. Christ entrusted His Word not to books, but to living men. They have transmitted it to their successors, and it is thus that it has come down to us through the vicissitudes of history, at once intact and living. In this sense, preaching is essentially tradition. Moreover, St. Irenaeus employs the two words as having the same meaning; kerygma and tradition with him are synonyms. Preaching thus refers not simply to a book, but to a book interpreted by the Church. To be still more precise, the Gospel is the crystallization of the preaching of the Apostles, and it is this preaching that is continued in the Church which is the heir of the Apostles.

This puts the preacher in his rightful place. He is charged by the Church to proclaim the message with which she herself is entrusted. He is essentially a messenger. As the Church is sent by Christ, the preacher is sent by the Church: 'And how can there be preachers, unless preachers are sent on their errand?'[1] Preaching in this sense is clearly a part of the priestly mission. It represents one of its essential functions, together with the offering of the sacrifice and the communication of the sacraments. And inasmuch as it is a mission, it represents an obligation. The Word must be proclaimed 'in season and out of season.' The message must be shouted in the ears of men. No sociological condition is required for the Word to be proclaimed, no other witness can be substituted for it.

One last element must be defined in order that we may understand the nature of preaching—that is, its object. What does the word say? Here again it is St. Paul who makes the matter clear. The word is the word of salvation,[2] the word of the Cross,[3] the word of reconciliation.[4] The object of the word is not a doctrine nor wisdom, as is the

---

[1] Rom. 10 [15].   [2] Acts 13 [26].   [3] 1 Cor. 1 [18].   [4] 2 Cor. 5 [19].

teaching of philosophers or sages. It is the proclamation
of an event, the Paschal event. It has only one object,
the Passion and Resurrection of Christ, considered as an
event decisive in history, as a divine action of cosmic
importance which overturns the universe. It consists in
announcing the incomprehensible richness of Christ,[1] by
which an era of grace is opened. It is the true object of the
Gospel to herald these tidings.

This event, which is at the same time judgement, creation,
and covenant, was already the object of the preaching of
the Prophets. They recall the great works of God in the past
history of Israel to lay the foundation for faith in the greater
work which God is to perform in the future.

'Do not remember those old things;
I mean to perform new wonders.'[2]

At the outset of the New Testament, St. John the Baptist
preaches repentance in view of the imminent Judgement:
'Already the axe has been put to the root of the trees.'[3] But
with the coming of Christ the promised event is present.
The Gospel does not tell us that there is a Paradise, but
that Paradise has come: 'To-day you will be with me in
Paradise.' And this event is essentially that of Easter.
It is the καιρός, the decisive moment of which Christ often
speaks. To this event the Apostles bear witness. St. John
replaces the word 'kerygma' by 'witness,' which indicates
that the object of the proclamation is an event already here.
It is the paradoxical character of the Gospel to proclaim
that the final, decisive event has taken place.

On the other hand, the decisive happening, the mysteries
of Christ are not only past. The Resurrection inaugurates
them, but they continue. We await the coming mystery

[1] Eph. 3 4.   [2] Isa. 43 18.   [3] St. Matt. 3 10.

which is the Parousia. Thus preaching is still the preaching
of repentance in view of the Judgement to come. The time
of the Church is the delay allowed by God who wishes
that all be saved.[1] And the content of this time is the
mission in which 'this gospel of the kingdom must first
be preached all over the world, so that all nations may hear
the truth; only after that will the end come.'[2] And finally
there is an actual mystery of the glorified Christ present
in the Church. The actions which He performs are sacramental actions, strictly divine actions, which continue the
great works of God in the two Testaments. Preaching is,
then, always a *Hodie*. It is the proclamation that here to-day
God is accomplishing His saving work. It is in this sense
an invitation to the sacrament, an invitation to baptism in
the missionary kerygma, an invitation to the Eucharist in
the homily of the Church. In the Sunday assembly the
liturgy of the Word precedes the liturgy of the sacrament,
as its very performance makes clear.

It should be added that between the three aspects of the
proclamation there is an organic relationship. It is this
very relationship that gives to preaching—and here in the
most practical sense of the word—its living structure.
Preaching is not, in fact, a logical exposition which only
convinces the mind. It must awaken the passions of the
soul, arouse desire, awaken faith, induce conversion.
It is here that the processes of sacred history come to join
the processes of the soul. Sacred history is not just merely
schoolmastering. The Old Testament arouses desire and
expectation, awakens desire for spiritual benefits. Confronted with these benefits the soul is overcome by despair,
so deeply does she feel herself powerless and unworthy.
The New Testament arouses hope. What God had accom-

---

[1] 2 Pet. 3 [9].   [2] St. Matt. 24 [14].

plished in Jesus Christ gives us the assurance that He can accomplish the same works in us. The essence of salvation is already fulfilled. Leaning on this hope, we must take the necessary measures to receive its fruits. And these measures we find embodied in the sacramental life, which renders us capable of a Christian life.

This leads to an essential aspect of preaching—its bond with the Christian Assembly. We have said that the Word of God is bound to the Christian community. Now the eucharistic assembly, and above all the Sunday Mass, is the visible expression of the Christian community, its concrete realization. It is then that the Word is most particularly present. This liturgy of the Word is essentially incorporated in the Mass of the catechumens. This first part is often neglected; it is not obligatory. People deliberately arrange to arrive after the sermon. In reality it constitutes a profound mystery. The Word of God is proclaimed officially by the Church in the reading of the Scriptures. It is not just simply a reading. It is the Word of God addressing itself directly to the community.

The preachers of the primitive Church were very much aware of this liturgical mystery of the Word. Just as, in the eucharistic liturgy, Christ is present under the forms of bread and wine, so He is present in an analogical sense, which is nevertheless real, under the forms of writing. One can speak in this way of a sacrament of Scripture. The first great preacher whose addresses we have preserved and who remains one of the greatest—Origen—said one day to his community: 'And now, if you wish, in this church and in this assembly, your eyes may behold the Lord. Indeed, when you direct the highest point of your soul to the contemplation of Wisdom and Truth, which is the only Son of the Father, your eyes behold Jesus. Happy is that community of whom it is written that the eyes of all, catechumens and faithful, men, women, and children, see Jesus not with the eyes of the body but with the eyes of the soul.'[1]

But this word of God, actually addressed to the Assembly, must be understood. The whole community hears this word, seeking its special meaning for itself. Preaching is, in this sense, a search made in common by the preacher and his hearers, praying together for the Holy Spirit, who alone gives understanding of the word. Origen sometimes pauses in his Homilies to invite the community to pray with him: 'On this question, if the Lord will enlighten my mind, thanks to your prayers (if we are in the least worthy to receive God's meaning), I will say a few words.'[2] Here we see how preaching is bound up with the actual out-pouring of the Spirit over the community, and how the preacher puts himself on the same level as the community. He, too, adopts an attitude of obedience.

But it remains true that this exposition of the Word of God comes back essentially to the preacher. Even if he is borne along by public prayer, it is still on him that the duty devolves of explaining Scripture. It is one of the functions of the priesthood. Origen says again, comparing the Christian preacher to the Hebrew priest: 'As the priest tears away the skin of the victim, so he releases the hidden meaning of the writing.'[3] The proclamation of the Gospel is a priestly office. And elsewhere: 'In the same way that the high priests, when they officiated had to make sure that the victim was without blemish, so that it would be agreeable to God, in the same way he who performs the sacrifice of the Gospel and proclaims the word of God must take care that there is no stain in his preaching, no

[1] *Hom. Luc.* 32.　　[2] *Hom. Ez.* IV, 3.　　[3] *Hom. Luc.* 14.

fault in his teaching, no error in his *magisterium*. And for this he must first offer himself for sacrifice, first render his members dead to sin, in order that not only by doctrine, but by the example of his life, he may bring it about that his oblation, accepted by God, procures the salvation of those that hear him.'[1]

Preaching in the heart of the Christian assembly carries a special grace. It is noticeable that for St. Paul it is when they gather together on the Lord's day that the charismata of prophecy, words of exhortation, wisdom, and instruction are given. Each Mass is a Pentecost. In particular, St. John tells us that the revelation of the Apocalypse was vouchsafed to him on the Lord's day.[2] This shows us that the mystical gifts of Christianity are given for the edification of the community. They are given within the community and for it. It is wrong to regard as opposed to each other, as is often done, the mystical and the liturgical, private prayer and prayer in church. In reality, in Christianity it is in the centre of worship, in the sacramental life, that the mystical life develops. This is its real setting. And its purpose is the growth of the Body of Christ.

Let no one say that this doctrine is inaccessible. It is even the experience of our own preaching. We all feel how much the problem of preaching, at the same time as it is a problem of doctrine, is also a problem of union with God, of inward docility of the spirit, of the spiritual meaning of the Scriptures. Certainly one need not wait to become a saint in order to preach. Who, then, would dare to do it? Moreover, it is not ourselves that we preach. But we are the first who need to understand the Word. When we preach, we are at one and the same time he who speaks and he who listens, he who judges and he who is judged.

[1] *Comm. Rom.* 10, 12.   [2] Apoc. 1 10.

It is to the extent that we share in the expectation of souls, and pray with them, that we make ourselves capable of understanding the word that will reach them through us.

This leads us to observe that preaching is also related to charity, another essential characteristic of the life of the Church. Preaching is a service to the community. This, too, is misunderstood to-day. There is, too, much insistance on material services rendered, on the witness of example. This is to forget that the first need of all souls is that one should speak to them of God. It is to forget that this word is not a human word, such as St. Paul condemns when he says that one should not only love in words, it is a grace, a divine *opus*, a duty for the people's sake to distribute this bread to those who hunger.

. . . . . .

The word leads to the Sacraments. These are pre-eminently the events which continue in the time of the Church, the great works of God in the Old and New Testaments. They have the same character. And it is by placing them within this continuity that the Fathers of the Church make them intelligible to us. Thus the first of these is baptism. Baptism is a new creation, in which the Spirit raises up from the waters the new man, just as He had raised up the first Adam, and had raised up again Jesus Christ. It is a liberation, in which the power of the same Word which had liberated the people who stood at bay by the sea, destined to extermination, and which had freed Christ from the bonds of death, frees the catechumen from that hopeless situation which is original sin. It is a covenant which allows the catechumen to enter into the covenant, made by the Word of God with human nature at the Incarnation, the eternal Covenant which repeats, but infinitely surpasses, the Covenant made with Moses.

Thus we always find ourselves again in the presence of those divine actions which always manifest the same modes of being. The goal of sacred history is to familiarize us with these divine ways, at the same time that they are working their effects in us. But these acts of God present a character which is in each case peculiar to each stage of sacred history, corresponding to the situation which each stage represents. Now the characteristic of the time of the Church is that it is one in which the salvation of the world, substantially brought about through Jesus Christ, is not yet manifested as it will be at the Parousia, and in which the action of God is exercised in the hidden world of hearts. It is neither solely expectation nor yet possession in entirety, but possession and expectation at the same time. 'We are sons of God even now,' says St. John, 'and what we shall be hereafter, has not been made known as yet;'[1] and St. Paul: 'Christ is your life, and when he is made manifest, you too will be made manifest in glory with Him.'[2]

This structure it is which we may call sacramental, and which corresponds to the present moment in the history of salvation. This time is that in which the great works of God are accomplished through those humble signs that are water, oil, and bread. Those who can only see the appearances see nothing there out of the ordinary, but nevertheless beneath these ordinary species are the celestial mysteries. For those who see things from outside, a little water is poured on the body, but that which is accomplished in baptism is as great as the creation of the world and the Resurrection of Christ. St. Ambrose tells us that the light which radiates from the baptized, mounting from the baptismal font and dressed in the robe of glory, is such that the angels cannot bear its brilliance.[3]

[1] 1 John 3 [2].   [2] Col. 3 [3-4].   [3] *On the Mysteries*, VII, 35.

No text can help us to show the continuity of the sacraments and the works of God in the Old and New Testaments better than the blessing of the baptismal water in the present ritual: 'O God, it is Thy Spirit who hovered over the waters at the creation of the world, as if to give them already the power to sanctify; it is Thou also, O God, who chastised the crimes of a guilty world in the down-pouring of the Deluge, and who thus gave an image of regeneration: because it was the same element which designated at once the destruction of sin and the birth of virtue. . . . It is thou, O water, which God made to spring forth in Paradise from the spring, and which He ordered to water the whole earth by four rivers; it is in the desert that He made thee flow from the rocks for a corrupt people; it is at Cana in Galilee that He changed thee to wine by a wondrous miracle of His power; it is in the Jordan that John gave Him thy baptism; it is from His side that He made thee flow at the same time as His blood.'

Let us consider these analogies. The first is that of the primordial waters sanctified by the Spirit. Just as the Spirit of God, hovering above the primaeval waters, raised up the first creation, so the same spirit, hovering over the baptismal waters, raises up a new creation, performs the work of regeneration. The Spirit is the Creator Spirit. The Word of Christ refers to this particular aspect: 'No man can enter into the kingdom of God unless birth comes to him from water.'[1] 'Why are you immersed in water?' Ambrose asks the catechumen. 'We read: The waters bring forth living souls.[2] And the living souls are born. That was done at the beginning of creation. But to you it is reserved that water should regenerate you through grace.'[3]

[1] St. John 3 [5].   [2] Gen. 1 [20].   [3] *On the Sacraments*, III, 3.

Already we can see the dimension which this analogy gives to baptism. It is of the same order as the creation of the world; and this because to create is an action truly divine. It is the same Spirit who raised up the first creation and who will raise up the new creation. The Spirit will descend on the waters of Jordan, there to raise up the new creation which is that of the Man-God. Baptism is the continuation in the time of the Church of this creative work. The very picture of springtime, in which baptism is given, expresses this analogy. As the spring is the yearly birthday of creation, it is also that of the new creation.

Immediately after the creation, the prayer of consecration makes a reference to the Deluge. Here it is a new action of God which appears, and a new symbol of water. No comparison is older than that between the Deluge and Baptism. It is already found in the First Epistle of St. Peter, in which baptism is called the anti-type of the Deluge. Optatus of Milevis writes in the fifth century: 'The Deluge is a type of baptism in the sense that the entire universe, polluted under the flood of sins, was restored to its first purity by the intervention of the waters.'[1] Water is the instrument of the judgement of God; it is water which destroys the sinful world. Baptism is a mystery of death. It is destruction of the old man, as the Deluge was destruction of the old world, so that a new creature might appear, washed clean by the renewal of the baptismal waters.

The essential point here is the symbolism of the water. Lactantius writes: 'Water is the symbol of death.'[2] And Ambrose: 'In water is the image of death.'[3] Father Lundberg has underlined the importance of the water of death, which to us appears strange;[4] but then we remember the

---

[1] *Donat.*, V, 1; P.L., XI, 1041.   [2] *Div. inst.* II, 10; P.L., VI, 311 A.
[3] *Sp. Sanct.*, 1, 6, 76; P.L. 16, 722 D.
[4] *La typologie baptismale dans l'Eglise ancienne*, pp. 64–166.

text of St. Paul, showing us that baptism is at once death with Christ and resurrection with Christ.[1] Now the prayer of consecration underlines the opposition between the creative waters and the waters of destruction, the Creation and the Deluge. 'It is the same element which shows at once the destruction of sin and the birth of virtue.' Thus the text of Paul is related to the baptismal rite itself. There it appears as a putting to death by immersion and a new birth by emersion. We find once more the authentic symbol of the rite, but by reference to the realities of the Old Testament.

With this, we are far from having exhausted the Biblical analogies of baptism. The prayer of consecration now speaks of the rivers of Paradise. Here is a new domain which we enter. No theme appears more frequently in the Patristic commentaries than that of the analogy between Adam's condition and the condition of the catechumen. Adam, after his sin, was driven forth from Paradise. Christ restored the thief to Paradise. Baptism is return to Paradise, which is the Church. From the beginning[2] the preparation for baptism appears as the anti-type of the temptation in the Garden. The rejection of Satan is for Cyril of Jerusalem the breaking of the pact which, since Adam, bound man to the devil. Baptism is truly, as we teach, the destruction of original sin. But the symbol is not that of the stain which the water effaces; it is the dramatic opposition of the exclusion from Paradise and the return to Paradise.

For baptism is a return to Paradise; and this theme is as essential to the liturgy as the Paschal theme. Christ is the

[1] Rom. 6 [4].
[2] See Jean Daniélou, 'Catéchèse pascale et retour au Paradis,' *Maison-Dieu*, 45 (1956), pp. 99–120.

new Adam, the first to return to Paradise. De Bruyne[1] and others have shown how the symbolism of ancient baptisteries is paradisal, with the trees of life and the four rivers. Cyprian writes: 'The Church, in the same way as in Paradise, contains within her walls trees laden with fruits. She waters these trees with the four rivers, by which she dispenses the grace of baptism.'[2] 'It is there,' adds Ephraem, 'that is gathered each day the fruit that gives life to us all.'[3] Nothing is older in the Church than this theme: it is in the *Odes of Solomon*, in the *Epistle to Diognetus*; Papias held it to be of Apostolic origin.

The prayer of consecration next refers to the rock in the desert. Here we are concerned with the Exodus cycle. We have first to reconsider a theme which is not in the prayer of consecration, but which appears in the *Exultet*, being one of the greatest importance—that of the crossing of the Red Sea. Already in the First Epistle to the Corinthians there is seen in this a type of baptism. We shall only cite one of the oldest Patristic attestations, that of Tertullian: 'When the people, freely leaving Egypt, escaped the power of Pharaoh and passed over the water, the water blotted out the king and all his army. What clearer figure of baptism can we give? The nations are liberated from the world, and that by water, and they leave the devil, who tyrannized over them in former times, obliterated by water.'[4]

Here too, it is important not to stop at symbols, but to look for the theological analogy. Tertullian shows this. In what does the great work of God, accomplished at the time of the passage through the Sea, consist? The people are in a desperate position, destined to extermination. By the power of God alone, the Sea divides, the people pass

---

[1] 'La décoration des baptistères paléo-chrétiens,' *Mélanges Mohlberg*, I, pp. 198 sqq.
[2] *Epist.* LXXIII, 10. [3] *Hymn. Par.*, VI, 9. [4] *Bapt.* 9.

through and reach the other side. They sing the song of deliverance. There is no question there of a work of creation, nor of a work of judgement, nor of a work of sanctification, but of a work of redemption, in the etymological sense of that word. God sets free—and only He can set free.

The situation of the catechumen is the same. He is at the edge of the baptismal font. His position is desperate. He is under the domination of the Prince of this world, and he is destined to death. It is then that by an act of the power of God alone the waters open, the catechumen crosses over them, and passing to the other side, having escaped the domination of the forces of evil, he too sings the canticle of the saved. Thus in both cases we are in the presence of a divine act of salvation, and here also, between the one and the other, intervenes the liberating power of Christ, the prisoner of death, who by the divine power had forced in that same Paschal night the iron bolts and the brazen locks to open, so that He might be the First-born of the resurrected.

The rock of the living waters brings us to quite another perspective. St. Paul also makes it a symbol of baptism: 'Our fathers . . . all drank the same prophetic drink, watered by the same prophetic rock which bore them company, the rock that was Christ.'[1] In the Old Testament, the outpouring of the living waters is promised at the end of time, united with the outpouring of the Spirit. And these texts of Ezechiel and Isaias are part of our actual liturgy of baptism. Now it is very probable, as Lampe has shown, that the baptism of John the Baptist refers to this prophecy, because he himself also unites the water and the Spirit.[2] It signifies that the eschatological time of the outpouring

---

[1] 1 Cor. 10 [4].   [2] *The Seal of the Spirit*, p. 25.

of the Spirit has arrived. And we know that this theme was dear to the community of Qumran. But John himself only baptized with water. It was Christ who poured out the water and the Spirit.

This it is which Christ Himself applies to Himself: 'If any man is thirsty, let him come to me, and drink; yes if a man believes in me, as the Scripture says, Fountains of living water shall flow from his bosom. He was speaking here of the Spirit . . . which had not yet been given.'[1] We may, with Cullmann,[2] recognize also the proclamation of baptism in those texts in John where the question of the living water is raised, particularly in the passage referring to the Samaritan woman. No doubt it is necessary with him and with tradition as a whole to recognize in the water and the blood springing from the side of Christ the image of the water united to the Spirit, because the blood is the symbol of the Spirit. Thus the crucified Christ is the eschatological Rock, from whose pure side springs the water that satisfies for ever, the baptism that gives the Spirit.

We may notice in this connexion that the gift of the Spirit is essentially linked with the outpouring of water. We meet in the third century a tendency to distinguish between the rite of water, which would purify, and another rite, unction, or the laying on of hands, which would give the Spirit. Gregory Dix relied on these texts in order to distinguish, in initiation, a sacrament of the Spirit, as distinct from baptism. But this is contrary to the primitive tradition, as it is to the common tradition. It is water, and water only, which in baptism gives the Holy Spirit. And the rites which accompany it are only illustrative. As to confirmation, that is a different sacrament, allied to spiritual growth and participation in the ministry.

[1] St. John 7 [37-39].   [2] *Les Sacrements dans l'Evangile johannique*, pp. 51-55, 81-84.

The Biblical themes that we have so far examined were concerned with water, but once again this is not the essential element in their relation with baptism. Equally the reference to water is secondary in a theme like that of the return to Paradise, where the emphasis is placed on the restoration of Adam to the life of grace to which God had destined him from the beginning, and to which baptism will restore him. What is more, the Eucharist takes its place just as much as baptism in this paradisal theme; and in any case both are strongly associated. In the same way, the rock of the living waters is related at the same time to baptism and the Eucharist.[1]

The essential thing is, in fact, the theological analogy. This appears in biblical themes other than those which tradition has applied to baptism and the Eucharist. One of these is the Covenant. Gregory of Nazianzus has expressly written: 'We must call the grace of baptism a covenant (διαθήκη).'[2] The Covenant is the act by which God pledges Himself to establish between man and Himself in an irrevocable manner a community of life. Christ fulfils the new and eternal Covenant by uniting for ever in Himself divine nature and human nature, in such a way that they may never be separated. We shall not forget that Covenant is one of the names for primitive Christianity, following Isaiah: 'I have made thee: Covenant of the people.'[3]

Now baptism has entered into this Covenant. It is baptism itself which constitutes it by the pledge of God and that of man. When baptism was given in an interrogative form, this pledge was made part of the very form of baptism, which was bestowed in faith and in water, as Justin

---

[1] See Jean Daniélou, *Sacramentum futuri*, pp. 169–73.
[2] *Patr. Gr.*, XXVI, 3680. [3] Isa. 42 [6].

says.[1] Later, this aspect is carried back to the pre-baptismal profession of faith: 'You too, catechumen, you must learn to understand the meaning of this saying: I renounce Satan. This saying is indeed a covenant (συνθηκή) with the Lord.'[2] This pledge is called σύμβολον, pact, and it is from this that the term passed to the baptismal profession of faith which goes before it. John Chrysostom underlines the unconditional and irrevocable character of God's pledge: 'God does not say: If this, that, or the other. Such were the words of Moses when he sprinkled the blood of the covenant. And God promises eternal life.'[3]

We note the reference to the blood of the Covenant sprinkled by Moses. The Old Covenant was sanctified by a sacrament, the sharing of the same blood, sprinkled over the people and the altar, signifying and effecting a communion of life. It is certainly in reference to this action of Moses that Christ, taking wine and blessing it, declares: 'This is my blood, the blood of the new covenant,' before sharing it among His disciples as a sign of communion of life effected between them and Him. The Eucharist is truly the new rite which succeeds the former agreement, and which at one and the same time attests and carries out the Covenant effected by Christ with humanity in the Incarnation and the Passion.

Here we see again all that the Biblical analogy implies. It gives eucharistic communion its full meaning as participation in the life of God, irrevocably won for humanity in Christ and offered to every man. It reunites the Eucharist with Scripture, and shows us the continuation in the time of the Church of the divine actions in the two Testaments.

[1] *Dial.*, CXXXVIII, 2.
[2] John Chrysostom, 'Catech. ad illumin.,' *P.G.*, XLIX, 239.
[3] *Co. Col.* 2, 6.

It illuminates the symbolism of the sacramental rites by showing in the sharing of blood the highest expression of the common gift of life, blood being the very expression of life.

As well as being at one and the same time a bond with God and in relation to this bond, the Covenant is also an incorporation into the people of God. This incorporation is expressed in the Old Covenant by circumcision. Cullmann, Sahlin and many others have shown the connexion between circumcision and baptism, and the precious element which it brings to the theology of baptism.[1] 'The baptism of the Christian was expressed in the circumcision of the Hebrews,' writes Optatus of Milevis.[2] But already the Epistle to the Ephesians underlines this parallelism: 'Remember, then, what you once were, the Gentiles, according to all outward reckoning. ... You were strangers to every covenant, with no promise to hope for. ... But now you are in Christ Jesus; now, through the blood of Christ, you have been brought close.'[3]

It is baptism which is the new rite which incorporates the people of God into the Church. As for other aspects, such as investiture and unction, there is a particular rite for these. It is the *sphragis*, the sign of the Cross marked on the forehead. Already Ezechiel had said that the members of the eschatological community bore on the forehead the *tau*, the sign designating Yahweh, the *Name* of Yahweh. It is probable that the Zadokites of Damascus bore this sign.[4] St. John's Apocalypse shows us the elect marked with the sign of Yahweh, that is, with the *tau*.[5] It is very probably the sign with which the early Christians were

[1] Oscar Cullmann, *Le baptême des enfants*, p. 45; Harald Sahlin, *die Beschneidung Christi*, p. 9; Jean Daniélou, Baptême et circoncision, *Mélanges Schmaus*, pp. 775–777.
[2] *Donat.*, V. 1; *P.G.*, XI, 1045 A.   [3] Eph. 2 [11-13].
[4] *Damascus Frag.* XIX, 19.   [5] Apoc. 7, 3, 14-1.

marked from the beginning in recognition of their member-
ship of the eschatological community, the New Covenant.
Now the sign had the form of the Cross. That is why, in a
Greek setting where its meaning was not understood, it is
interpreted as the Cross of Christ. But Hermas says again:
'Those who are marked with the Name.'[1]

The Eucharist in its turn is an aspect of contemporary
sacred history, a wondrous work of God. Similarly the
Liturgy is inscribed within the movement of sacred history.
The Preface is a thanksgiving for the great works performed
by God in the past. The old Eastern Prefaces recall the
great works of God, the creation of the sun and the stars, of
the fish and the birds, the wonderful creation of man, the
mighty works accomplished by Yahweh among the people
of Israel, the still more wonderful works accomplished by
the Trinity in Jesus Christ.

Just as the Prophets only recall the great acts of God
in the past in order to establish confidence in the more
wondrous works that He will accomplish in the future, so
the Preface only recalls the great works of God (no longer
just in the Old Testament, but now also in the New) in
order to establish confidence in the power of God to
perform His wondrous works, not only in the future
but in the present time of sacred history, in the life of the
new people of God. This is the very movement and
exemplary form of the prayer which is thanksgiving and
supplication, anamnesis and epiclesis. The greatness of all
that God has accomplished in the past is the guarantee of
what He can accomplish in the present, in the eucharistic
καιρός.[2]

---

[1] *Similitudes* IX, 13, 2. See Jean Daniélou, 'Le signe de la croix,' *Table Ronde*,
120 (1957), pp. 35–38.
[2] See Jean Daniélou, 'Le καιρός de la messe chez saint Jean Chrysostome,'
Mélanges Jungmann, pp. 71–78.

Now this epiclesis,[1] this petition, has an exact bearing on the three great aspects of sacred history of which we have just spoken—the presence of the glorified Christ, the accomplishment of His redemptive work, the giving of actuality to the Church. Its object is first the presence of the glorified Christ beneath the species of bread and wine. This again is a mighty work of God, an essential aspect of present sacred history. The Church, against all forms of rationalism, affirms it as transubstantiation, thus designating this action as truly divine, absolutely disconcerting to our minds, making that which was bread and wine the true body and blood of Christ.

Here we are confronted again with one of those thresholds—we have already met several others—which mark our passing from the level of sense-experience to that of spiritual reality. And the difficulty of this transition is that it always arouses a tendency to separate the two domains, to divide once more the Christ of history from the Christ of faith. So it was with the empty tomb and the Resurrection of Christ, so, too, with the visible Church and the action of the risen Christ, so now with the bread and wine and the risen body of Christ. The human mind seeks to make a radical distinction between the two levels, to abandon to history, sociology, or physics all that is in line with the material level and shows itself absolute master there—and to confine to mere faith whatever presents a supernatural character. Thus there would be on one side the man Jesus and on the other the Word of God; on one side the fate of His dead body and on the other His spiritual presence in the risen appearance; on one side the establishment of the Church and her vicissitudes, and on the other the action of Christ in souls; on the one side the bread and

[1] We mean by *epiclesis* the whole of the prayer of consecration in the traditional sense.

wine and on the other the presence of Christ in the assembly.

But the mystery is precisely that the Word *was* made flesh. It is not necessary to be a Christian to suppose that God is God and man is man. But to believe that God is man and man God, that is the very essence of Christianity. This may well seem like confusing the two domains. Yet it is God Himself who confounds the two, or better still, who comes and confounds the demands of our reason in order to introduce us to ways that are His. Now we have said from the beginning of this book that the essential point of the mystery of Christ is the rigorous continuity He presents in all His states, and which makes Him belong not successively to separate domains, but simultaneously to all these domains, so as to fill them all. It is an illusion which makes us regard as an autonomy of our reason that which is no more than a defeat of our reason, which makes us see as an autonomous nature that which is only a form of a historical nature, which hinders us from accepting this outgrowth of a mystery which remains a mystery even on the level of phenomenal experience.

Thus Christ performs the actions of a man. 'We have touched Him with our hands,' says St. John.[1] And He who performs these actions is the Incarnate Word. Thus it is the same body which Magdalen placed as a corpse within the tomb, and which appears to her in a risen form. Thus our eyes continue to see the bread and wine; and nevertheless the bread and wine is the body and blood of Christ. It is here that our reason is confronted by the supreme paradox. 'These words are hard.'[2] Here, too, our reason encounters a break in the very pattern of the appearances, through which a ray of divine light passes,

[1] I St. John I [1].   [2] St. John 6 [60].

and without which it would remain enclosed in the world of appearances. It is this that restrains us from dividing our lives into two parts, from being on the one hand men, and on the other hand Christians. This is the scandal and the good news of the Incarnation.

It is much easier to contrast a phenomenal world with a noumenal world, corresponding with each other without overlapping. This is what Bultmann and Duméry do. It is, in fact, what the Gnostics did. They already recognize two Christs, the Jesus of the Kenoma and the Only Begotten of the Pleroma. It is the eternal and continual temptation. Kant merely provided it with a metaphysical formula. According to this, there is a noumenal Christ whom we attain by faith and a phenomenal Jesus existing in history. But unfortunately the tomb is empty and the body has not been found. The matter is then of no importance. Then why do the Evangelists make so much of it? There is the scandal—but there is the faith. There is only one Jesus, God and man, earthly and heavenly. This is not a confusion of levels, but a union of natures. Here is precisely the very essence of the Incarnation. For the Manhood is not the Godhead. But the same person is God and man. Thus there is only one Eucharist, the Body of Christ and the species of bread.

This eucharistic presence of the risen Christ is part of the sacramental economy, inasmuch as it is the summing-up of contemporary sacred history. Indeed we have said that the first aspect of the action of the Word in the time of the Church is the glorious Manhood of Christ, which itself constitutes the permanent source in which all grace is a participation. Thus the Eucharist is not just the presence of the working of Christ, nor the presence of the institution of the Church, but it is first of all the presence of the glorified

Manhood of Christ. It is in this sense that the Eucharist is truly the fullness of the mystery which is present, contained in the sacrament. It would present only a mutilated image if it did not bear within it the primordial gift, the principle of the new creation.

Christ is present in other respects in the priestly action which makes Him the mediator between God and man. It is this priestly action which is made present in the Mass. The Mass is thus the sacrifice, the supreme act of worship, by which God is perfectly glorified, and of which the sacrifice of Abel, Abraham, and Melchisedech were the first outlines. This act of worship is henceforth the only acceptable form of worship. It is by this action that all glory rises up again to the Father. *Per ipsum et cum ipso et in ipso est tibi, Deo Patri omnipotenti, omnis honor et gloria.* This is why that action has official, universal character, marked by the presence of angels, which the end of the Preface calls upon, thus showing in the Mass the presence of the heavenly liturgy.

The Eucharist is secondly the communication of grace through contact with the Body of Christ. And here another aspect of the matter needs to be considered. The Mass does not repeat the self-same actions of Christ in His Passion, Resurrection and Ascension. These actions have been accomplished once and for all, and could not be repeated. But the sacraments render them present in their supernatural efficacy. This is true in the first place of baptism. As St. Cyril of Jerusalem rightly said, this is an imitation of the death of Christ which bestows its saving effect. In other words, the event which it constitutes is not the death and Resurrection of Christ, but the death and Resurrection of the Christian, which are the fruit of the death and Resurrection of Christ. Methodius thus shows us the perpetual birth of the Church in the sacraments which spring from the wounded side of Christ. 'In our baptism, we have been buried with him,' says St. Paul.[1]

What baptism performs in a rudimentary fashion, the Eucharist brings to its fulfilment. It appears here under a new aspect. It also plunges the Christian into the death and Resurrection of Christ. In this respect its effect is no different from that of baptism. But what baptism does inchoately, the Eucharist comes forward to continue and perfect. The shared bread and wine are the efficacious signs of the New Covenant which signifies and activates at once in the soul and body of the Christian the communion of life which is established in the Incarnate Word between the Word and human nature, and whose saving effect they renew in every Christian. 'This is the chalice of my blood, the blood of the new testament.' Thus the Eucharist fulfils for every soul the nuptial mystery first accomplished in the Incarnation and in the Church.

The *res* of the Eucharist is, thus, as St. Thomas has emphatically stated, the mystical Body. It is through it that the Body of Christ is formed until God is all in all. The proper effect of the sacrament is, then, to render actual the action by which Christ builds up His Body. It is remarkable that these two aspects are present in the Eucharist; it renders present Christ the Head of the mystical Body, and it renders present the action which builds up that mystical Body. Each communion is thus a wonderful work of God which brings about the transformation of Christians into Christ, until all that is mortal is absorbed by life. The Eucharist is the action by which he who has been grafted by baptism into the mystical Vine receives the divine influx which makes him bear much fruit. It is the

---

[1] Rom. 6 [4].

burning coal which consumes all that is mortal, and communicates the incorruptible life of the Spirit.

Thus, being the actual presence of the glorified Manhood of Christ, the Eucharist is, with baptism, the actual presence of His divinizing activity. It is also, as the summing up of the whole economy of the action of the Trinity, the actual presence of the Church. For it is in the eucharistic assembly that the Risen Christ shows Himself present; and His sacramental presence is bound up with the eucharistic assembly. Thus the mystery of the Bride and Bridegroom is concretely fulfilled within the context of each Eucharist. And it is by participation in the marriage of the Bride and the Bridegroom that the union of the soul with her Spouse is accomplished. The presence of the Church is necessary to that union. As the Son does nothing without the Father, Christ does nothing without the Church. Her presence is necessary in all His actions. There is no sacramental action that is not of the Church.

. . . . .

Thus the Church appears as the visible institution which is officially and exclusively charged by Christ to spread throughout the world the saving work which He first accomplished in His Person. It remains for us to show that this mission is the common work of the whole Church. But we must first define what we mean by the official character of that mission. The Apostle, says the Second Epistle to the Corinthians, has the function of an ambassador.[1] He is an official envoy, furnished with full powers. He is invested with an authority that gives him full right to speak and to act. This is at once his greatness and his limitation. He is only the representative of a higher authority. The authority which he represents is that of the

[1] 2 Cor. 5 20.

Church. And the authority of the Church is itself a communication from God.

The first mission, which is the bed-rock of every enterprise, is the sending of the Word by the Father. This Trinitarian spring is the spring of every mission. The word 'mission,' by which we denote in the Church the sending of the missionary, is the very same that theology uses for the coming of Christ and the coming of the Spirit into the world. Indeed we distinguish, in the Holy Trinity, on the one hand, the relationships of the divine Persons amongst themselves, which are internal to the life of the Trinity, and, on the other hand, the external operations of the divine Persons, in Creation and in Redemption. These operations are called missions; in other words, the Father sends the Son, and the Father and the Son in their turn send the Spirit.

The origin of mission, the primordial mission, is this: *In principio erat Verbum*, and next: *Et Verbum caro factum est*. It is the coming of the Word of God in the flesh. It constitutes the hidden design of God from all Eternity, of which the world never had any suspicion. No system of philosophy and no religion has ever foreseen that God would thus come among men and become, in the very midst of mankind, the source of the divine life. 'As the Father has sent me,' says our Lord.[1] 'My meat is to do the will of him who sent me.'[2] And again, in the high-priestly prayer: 'As my Father sent me into the world, I also in my turn send them into the world.'[3] That is why Christ behaved as an ambassador. An ambassador is one who acts in the name of another, who is charged with a mission, who has very precise instructions for the accomplishment of some task. He therefore does not act in his own name.

[1] St. John 20 21.   [2] St. John 4 34.   [3] St. John 17 18.

He comes essentially to perform a task that has been entrusted to him, utterly dependent upon him who sends him. And the faithful ambassador is he who brings to its completion the mission that has been entrusted to him. 'I do nothing of myself, but that which the Father has shown me, that do I.'[1]

In Christ the whole mystery of the missionary is already present, and the contemplation of Christ in His missionary activity makes us understand the meaning of all missionary activity, of that total dependence of the missionary in relation to Him who sends him. From the very moment when the missionary does his own work, he is no longer a missionary, he is acting on his own authority, he is no longer clothed in the authority of Him who sends him. That is why, for example, when a Christian, instead of preaching Christ and being the servant of the Word, preaches himself, and his own theories, and substitutes these for the revelation of Christ, and no longer lives in obedience to Christ and the Church, from that moment he loses his authority, and his activity loses all its value.

As the Father sent the Son, so in His turn the Son sends the Apostles. This is the second expansion of the missionary movement, springing from the heart of God, springing from the heart of the Father. This second expansion of the missionary movement is that by which Christ, sent by the Father, in His turn sends His Apostles. 'As the Father has sent me, so also I send you.'[2] It is very important to notice, as we have said, that in the Gospel Christ devoted almost the whole of His life, not only to being a missionary, but to forming missionaries. It is to the Church that He entrusted the evangelizing of all nations, equipping her with powers that make her capable of exercising

---

[1] St. John 5 [19].   [2] St. John 20 [21].

His ministry. And it is at Pentecost that the mission of the Apostles took shape by the coming together of the training which Christ had given them, in some sense from without, with the inward mission of the Holy Spirit who now descends upon them so as to quicken them with a divine power.

We may say, then, that mission is essentially a divine work. It is the proper work of the Word and the Spirit. It is the Word of God and the Spirit of God working in the world; thus it is not a human work, and consequently men are never more than its servants and its instruments. In proportion as we are missionaries in one way or another, we share in a work which is not our own, and by the same token we must accept the commands that are those of God and the Church, precisely because we are merely those who have to carry out these missions, who must accomplish these tasks with the same dependence with regard to the Church as Christ showed in relation to His Father. Here we find a great mystery of dependence and obedience, an obedience, moreover, which is essentially an 'obedience of love,' namely the need which Christ had of being hidden in the will of His Father, and which causes us too to experience the need to be hidden within the will of Christ, the will of the Church. This is not an obedience which is extrinsic, but an obedience which leaves our initiative free for adaptation and invention. Just as Christ reveals a marvellous initiative, a wonderful independence in the work of the Kingdom of God, and at the same time a perfect dependence in relation to His Father, so obedience to the Church is freedom of invention, Apostolic creation, but within an inward dependence, strict and loving, by its bond with the Spirit dwelling in the Church.

Mission has for its object the entirety of those means by

which the life and growth of the Church are assured. It is thus the Church in her dynamic aspect which it leads us to consider. We must begin here from the most general aspect, which is precisely the one that will enable us to understand mission as a combined operation, because it is the work of the Church. We are all in the service of a common task, and it is this identity of the end pursued that demands convergence of the means employed. By a kind of paradox, but which nevertheless expresses an essential truth, we must say that the whole Church is in the service of the whole Church, because the Church is at once the beginning and the end, the point of departure and the point of arrival, the form and the life.

Let us be more precise. Something forms itself in our midst which is the work of God, the *opus Dei*. *Pater meus operatur et ego operor*.[1] But in this building up of the Body of Christ, God calls for our co-operation. It is not accomplished without us. We have here an active role. The Church is at once that which we create and that which creates us. The whole Church is the work of the whole of Christendom. We remember the words of Dostoievsky: 'Each is responsible for all before all.' St. Paul has described this growth of the body under that which first flows from the Head, which is Christ, but not without the co-operation of the members, who are the Christians. 'It is on Christ that all the body depends; it is organized and unified by each contact with the source which supplies it; and thus, each limb receiving the active power it needs, it achieves its natural growth, building itself up through charity.'[2] The work is God's work. But in this work each must co-operate. Every Christian is a fellow-worker with God.

This co-operation of the whole body in its own growth

[1] St. John 5 [17].   [2] Eph. 4 [16].

presents two aspects, personal and functional. We understand by this personal aspect the co-operation that every
Christian brings to the growth of the body by the intensity
within him of the supernatural life of charity. The ministries
are all different, but there is one gift preferable to all others
in which it behoves each one of us to be strong, and that is
love. This is the doctrine of the communion of saints, of
the revertibility of merits, which holds a central place in
the Catholic faith. Perhaps in early Christianity it had a
greater meaning than in ours, this personal participation
of all Christians, and pre-eminently of contemplatives, in
the growth of the Church. Karl Rahner has shown, in a
series of articles on Origen,[1] how for early Christianity the
reconciliation of sinners appears as the combined work of
the Bishop who performs it sacramentally and of the faithful
who perform it mystically.

We do not wish to insist on this point. The other inter-
ests us more—the functional aspect of the co-operation
of the body in its own building-up. From this aspect no
member of the body is excluded. There is a participation
of the laity in all the ministries of the Church, in its teaching
function, in its sacramental life, even in its government.
But in this realm the hierarchy, and above all the episcopate, holds an absolutely privileged position. All co-operation of this order in the building up of the Church
will always be carried out in an attitude of dependence
so far as the episcopate is concerned, and will always
remain secondary in respect to them. This is the doctrine
of St. Paul: there are diversities of functions in the unity
of charity.

It is in this perspective of functional or ministerial co-

[1] 'La penitence chez Origène,' *RSR.* 37 (1950), pp. 252–86.

operation in the work of God that a theology of the priesthood, which means especially the episcopate, is most
happily defined. This is true of its origin. Jesus devoted
an important part of His earthly life to the education of the
Apostolic college, the nucleus of the episcopal college.
It is to this college that He confided the divine powers
which are His. It is He who sent them throughout the
entire world to promulgate the good news and gather all
men into the Church. It is upon it that the Holy Spirit
was directly poured out on the day of Pentecost. To it,
Christ confided the secrets of His design in the Discourse
after the Last Supper. It is to be the effective inspiration
of the mission.

This remains true of the actual Church. The episcopal
college, gathered round the successor of Peter, is the supreme
instrument, on the level of the ministry, of the building
up of the Body of Christ. It carries full responsibility for
this. It is invested by the Blessed Trinity with a permanent
and universal mission. At every instant it is appealing to
the whole of humanity, preaching conversion in view of
the Judgement to come. This mission is a strict duty of
obedience which must be performed under all circumstances in the midst of contradictions and crises. It is a
mandate for which account will be demanded. It has a
universal character; that is to say, it is not only a responsibility for the Christians of a diocese, but a responsibility
for all men, Christians and otherwise, since the knowledge
of salvation concerns all. The episcopate is Catholic in the
strict sense of the word.

This mission is properly a service, a ministry. The work
is that of God. Priesthood is a dispensation of the mysteries, that is to say, service in the economy of salvation.

And we find here at the functional level the central idea of co-operation. The work is that of the Holy Spirit. The priesthood is the dispenser of that work. No one has put this aspect in better relief than Gregory of Nazianzus. He describes the design of God, which is the restoration of the image of God in man: 'To this were leading the educative Law, the Prophets who mediated between the Law and Christ, and Christ Himself who fulfils and ends the Law.'[1]

But if this functional co-operation in the building up of the Body of Christ exists above all in the episcopate, the totality of the Church is associated with it, in union with, and dependence on, the episcopate. This latter is first of all associated directly with the priesthood, to whom it communicates its power and jurisdiction. It associates with this the laity, on whom it confers a special mission in the appropriate order of the spiritual building up of the mystical Body, and which constitutes Catholic Action in the widest sense of the word. We must not fail to recognize the place of a whole series of ministries, intermediary between the priesthood and the laity, and which held an important place in the primitive Church—deacons, readers, and others. We are aware that the question of the restoration of these ministries is being discussed to-day.

Thus, under the ministerial aspect, the building up of the Body of Christ still appears as a common task. No element in the Church is in this order merely passive. And it would be to misunderstand the legitimate contrast between the Church which teaches and the Church which is taught, if we were to regard it as merely the contrast between an active and a passive element. It emphasizes only that the

[1] *P.G.*, XXXV, 432 B.

power to teach resides pre-eminently in the hierarchy, but it is all Christians who, in very diverse degrees, are called upon to play here an active part in the building up of the Body of Christ. All Christians are called to missionary work.

. . . . .

The first difficulty we encountered in our exploration of the mystery of Christ was the transition from the Christ of history to the Christ of faith. And it seemed to us that the objective study of the datum of the New Testament showed us the impossibility of dissociating one from the other, and that the Christ of history is like the visible seal of the reality of the Christ of faith. Then there appeared another difficulty, that of the relation of the Christ of faith to the Christ of the Church. For many men, the principal difficulty is that they must pass through the Church in order to come to Christ. And Protestantism in particular appears as an expression of the attempt to be united directly with Christ without passing through the Church.

The continuation of our inquiry showed us that this position was also untenable. On the one hand, the Church appears as strongly bound to the Christ of history, if it be true that the public life of Jesus was devoted principally to laying her foundations. No one to-day would accept Loisy's thesis, according to which Christ was only the Prophet of the imminence of Judgement. And if it be true that she is at once the place where the risen Christ is present under the appearance of bread and wine, and that she is in another respect the very object of the action of the risen Christ, the temple made of living stones which is built throughout history on the rock that is Christ, still more does the Church appear bound to the Christ of faith.

BIBLIOGRAPHY

O. CULLMANN, *Les sacrements dans l'Évangile johannique*, Paris, 1951.

ST. AMBROSE, *Des Sacrements, des mystères*, Paris, 1950.

ST. JOHN CHRYSOSTOM, *Huit catéchèses baptismales*, Paris, 1957.

JEAN DANIÉLOU, *Bible et Liturgie*, Paris, 1951.

M. LOT-BORODINE, *Un maître de la spiritualité byzantine au XIVe siècle: Nicolas Cabasilas*, Paris, 1958.

O. CASEL, *Le mystère du culte*, Paris, 1944.

Y. CONGAR, *Jalons pour une theologie du laïcat*, Paris, 1954.

CHAPTER VIII

THE INWARD MASTER

THE personal encounter of the soul with Christ constitutes precisely the opposite pole to the scriptural testimony concerning the earthly life of Jesus. It is at these opposite poles that our approaches to Christ differ most widely, and there is the greatest temptation to isolate them one from the other. Thus, for history, Christ is merely the person of whom the Gospel speaks. He cannot be a personal 'event.' On the other hand, there are those for whom only the inward event has any importance, and the very existence of the historical Christ comes to be regarded as of secondary value. Our whole purpose is to show the impossibility of separating the two approaches. We cannot be content with a mere biography of Jesus, nor with the mere experience of Christ.

The different viewpoints which we have examined are precisely those that compel us to avoid any separation. Between Jesus the historical personality and Christ the inward event, unity is established by Christ the centre of history. It is He who prevents us from reducing the life of Christ to a mere historical episode, and who reveals in that life the fulfilment of the decisive event in history, and endows it with the significance of a mystery. It is He also who forbids us to reduce the personal encounter with Christ to a subjective experience, but connects it with the presence of the glorified Christ in the Church. Thus from the Incarnation of the Word to the transfiguration of the soul, we are confronted by the same story, that of the works of the Word, whose Incarnation marks the first act, whilst the divinization of the soul will be the final act.

It remains true, however, that the story of the personal encounter between Christ and the soul recapitulates the various stages of the story of the action of the Word within mankind. Pierre Courcelle has shown that according to St. Augustine the soul first discovers the action of the Word in its personal history, in the sequence of graces which have led it to conversion; this corresponds to the 'Confessions.' Afterwards the soul discovers the action of the Word in universal history, in the series of stages from the Creation to the Session at the right hand; this corresponds to the 'City of God.'[1] Thus we shall find, at the level of the great works of God in the soul, the same ways that we have found in the great works of God in history. It is this that justifies the application to the spiritual life, by Origen or St. John of the Cross, of types from the Old Testament or events from the New.[2] Everything depends on the same Trinity acting in the same ways.

Now the work of the Word in history consists in the first place in the act by which the love of God searches for man in the place where he is, takes hold of him in all his wretchedness, and makes a new reality come into being where there was none before. The initiative remains entirely with Love. This is also true of the activity of the Word at the personal level. It is one of its essential aspects: 'It was not you that chose me, it was I that chose you.'[3] This is the vital point which St. Augustine defended with unmistakable emphasis against every kind of Pelagianism and semi-Pelagianism. It touches indeed upon the very heart of Christianity, which, let us say once more, is the movement of God towards man before being the movement of man towards God.

[1] *Recherches sur les Confessions de Saint Augustin*, pp. 13–27.
[2] This is misunderstood by R. P. C. Hanson, *Allegory and Event*, p. 281.
[3] St. John 15 [16].

Thus the meeting of the soul with Christ, which is conversion, is preceded by a meeting of Christ with the soul, which alone makes conversion possible. The action of the Word in the soul accordingly consists in the first place of lengthy preparations in which the grace of God comes seeking man, dead as he is in spiritual death, to bring to life within him the first promptings of goodwill, enabling him to rise up and walk. The search for God is the first gift of grace. But the soul only seeks for God because God has sought for it. This first search will be able to do no more than to set about to find. But it represents that early stage of obscure groping which is the initial response to the activity of the Word.

Thus the pagan world still remains at the level of the Advent of Christ, in the time of waiting. But this does not mean that it is a stranger to the action of the Word. If the Church is the place whence the lifegiving powers of the risen Christ are radiated, the action of the Word reaches out to the farthest limits of mankind simply to guide these men into the Church, so that they may be quickened by the risen Christ. The Church is, as it were, the very heart and centre of God's activity in the world. This activity reaches out to the limits. It is controlled entirely at the centre, as an organized preparation. Without it men would never reach the centre, were it not that their turning towards God is already an action of His.

Conversion then, in its turn, is equally a work of the Word. If, as St. Augustine says, He works in us without us, then the very next thing we do, we cannot do it without Him. 'Thus in every way,' says St. Paul, 'the primacy was to become his.'[1] This is true of the whole economy; and it is also true of the individual economy. If the beginning

[1] Col. 1 18.

is His initiative, all growth is also His initiative, and final perseverance will also be His doing. Thus an essential feature of the ways of God appears in the life of grace. And it is in this manner that sacred history enables us to understand our personal pilgrimage. Its laws are the same. The property of the spiritual—to paraphrase Wordsworth— is to give us a consciousness of the more, where there was no knowledge of the less. This is, strictly speaking, creative action, which is pure increase. The property of grace, which is in the beginning that of making something where there was nothing, of making life spring up where death reigned, always remains that of bringing to life more than was given before—'grace answering to grace,' as St. John says.[1]

It is this that once more establishes the spiritual life as sacred history, and distinguishes it from the various types of philosophical spirituality. These involve man's rediscovery of himself as estranged from himself in the world of appearances. There is, then, a kind of human reality which is subsistent, the inward man, veiled by the life of appearance. As soon as this life of appearance is made to go, man becomes once more what he is. It is a question of being converted to oneself, of rediscovering oneself in one's true reality which had been lost. The individual theme is the same as the collective theme. It always consists of a primordial reality which only has to be rediscovered, not in any realm of history, but in an escape from history, as if time has never done anything save to mar an original perfection.[2]

The spiritual life of the Christian, on the other hand, is real history. It does not consist of rediscovering oneself,

[1] St. John 1 [16].
[2] Cf. W. K. C. Guthrie, *In the Beginning: Some Greek views on the origins of life and the early state of man*, 1957.—Trans.

but of surpassing oneself, because one is seized by Another, who alone can raise us above ourselves. It presupposes this action of love, and relies upon that love. Its foundation is faith, not knowledge. It is not primarily a question of knowing oneself, as Socrates required, but of knowing Jesus Christ. The spiritual life is an invitation to an unknown gift, not a rediscovery of one's unrecognized riches. It is a continual giving, a continual increase. So the essential attitude which it demands is consciousness of fundamental need. 'Separated from me, you have no power to do anything.'[1] This poverty is still there in the midst of plenty, yet as soon as grace is accepted, it is lost. This does not mean that grace is not given permanently; the very permanence of the gift is, as we have said, itself the mark of the ways of the God of the Covenant.

This is shown by the fact that there is always in God's gift an element of permanence and also of actuality. It is both something which persists and something which happens. The grace given at baptism confers both character and sanctification. As character, it provides a permanent claim to grace. As sanctification, it operates here-and-now. But the character bestowed is also a grace. It is never a right, or else it is a right that has been conceded. Grace, in fact, by making us sons gives us a right of inheritance. But to be a son is the first of graces, and always remains a grace, an entirely free gift. The inheritance is not due to our nature. As natural men we have no rights at all, and the rights we have are only the result of that first act of grace which was adoption. It may be open to us to withdraw from sanctification, from the blessings of grace. But it is not open to us to blot out the character; we remain baptized. And, sinners though we have been, we do not have

[1] St. John 15 [5].

to be baptized again; it suffices that we should return to God and offer Him that claim to grace which is the baptismal character, for Him once more to bestow upon us His promised sanctification.

We can see, then, that the spiritual life is a continual progress in faith, as Gregory of Nyssa and John of the Cross recognized: 'To go towards that which thou knowest not, thou must needs pass through that which thou knowest not.' The temptation is to want to walk in the light of one's own experience, for no one ever wishes to go beyond the boundaries of his experience. But the spiritual life consists entirely of being led by God into ways which are foreign to our experience. The pattern of the Christian, as Jean Hering has well said, is not the princess who is sent into exile and longs to return, it is Abraham who sets out for an unknown country which God is to show him.[1] Scripture says indeed: 'He left his home . . . without knowing where his journey would take him.'[2]

It is not, therefore, upon her own experience that the soul can rely. She is journeying towards a foreign country. She relies solely upon the promise of God. It is this dispossession of the soul, which makes her no longer rely in any way upon herself, but entirely upon God, in which the essential disposition of the spirit consists. This does not mean that nothing is gained. Christ is a way on which we move forward. But what is gained is unimportant compared with what is awaited, 'a drop of the night-dew gleaming in the Bridegroom's locks,' as Gregory of Nyssa[3] puts it. And by the side of the infinity of the divine darkness, as Gregory again expresses it, the Bridegroom says, 'Get thee up, to her who has already arisen. And thus the soul

---

[1] *Le Royaume de Dieu et sa venue*, p. 150.   [2] Heb. 11 [8].
[3] *Commentary on the Canticle*; P.G., XLIV, 1004 A.

moves forward from beginnings to beginnings through beginnings that have no end.'[1]

Each of these beginnings is truly initiated by the Word. They are the visitations of the Word, of which St. Bernard speaks. Thus is the spiritual life made up of these successive acts of the Word. The first was the original call, coming to look for the dead soul, a complete stranger to God, and saying to her, Arise; for by comparison with the road that lies ahead, she is not yet alive. This new call is that of conversion. It corresponds to a stage at which the soul, awakened to spiritual reality by the Word, enters into a Covenant with God, in which obedience to the Word becomes decisive. This it is which corresponds, in the pilgrimage of the non-Christian, to the combination of the catechumenate and baptism, and finds its expression in the σύνταξις, the baptismal symbol, the free and final obedience to faith. And this is what, in the baptized child, will be the free ratification of a gift already received and personally accepted.

⊢ Conversion and baptism are thus an end. They are felt to be such. They are the unfolding of a whole sequence of graces which the convert can look back upon, and which have marked the successive stages that have led him to his decision. Thus he already has behind him an entire sacred history, a whole series of acts of the Word. Nevertheless this fruition is only a beginning. The first stages of grace have brought the soul to baptism. But baptism is a point of departure. It communicates supernatural life to the soul, but it does so in an inchoate fashion. The spiritual life is to be, as Dom Marmion says, 'the blossoming of those perceptions which derive from our divine adoption.' Immersed in Jesus Christ, the soul must be transformed into Him.

[1] *Commentary on the Canticle*; P.G., XLIV, 876 B, 941 C.

Now the transformation of the soul into Jesus Christ is the work of Jesus Christ. Through baptism the soul becomes the sanctuary where the Trinity dwells 'in a very deep abyss,' as St. Teresa says.[1] This expresses one of the aspects of the mystery of the Covenant, which was the dwelling of Yahweh in the Temple and the dwelling of the Word in the Manhood of Christ. It is the mark of an abiding presence. This indwelling is connected with grace itself inasmuch as it has a permanent character. For grace is the sharing in the life of the Trinity which expresses an especially close relationship with the Trinity. It is inasmuch as the Trinity sets grace to work in the soul that the Trinity dwells there. It is therefore the expression of this new relationship established by grace between the soul and the Word.

However, this can be expressed in a different way: 'You have only to live on in me, and I will live on in you.'[2] We can say that the Trinity dwells in the soul, or we can say that the soul dwells in the Trinity. In the latter case, the vital fact is that the depths of the soul are already sounded in the silent profundity of the Trinity, into which the Manhood of Christ entered at the Ascension, and to which it attracts the soul that is united with it. In a noteworthy passage, St. Paul says in effect that through baptism we are risen with Christ and seated with Him in the heavens.[3] Thus in baptism we share in Christ's Ascension. It is not only in expectation that we are with Him in the heavens. Grace is already an actual sharing in the divinization of Christ's Manhood. This is one of the points on which the Catholic theology of grace is maintained in opposition to forensic justification.

This twofold aspect—the dwelling of God in ourselves

[1] *Interior Castle*, 7th Mansion.   [2] St. John 15 [4].   [3] Eph. 1 [20].

223

and the dwelling of us in God—indicates the point at which the spiritual life passes beyond all images, and reveals the paradoxical character which masters of the spiritual life have emphasized. It is at once light and darkness, rapture and restraint, motion and rest. From our present standpoint, it is the entry of the soul into herself, not to find herself, but to find there the Word who dwells in her in a very deep abyss. Thus the spiritual life is inwardness, in the sense of conversion from the apparent world to the real world where God is the Inward Master. Thus is the soul for ever sought after by the Word who dwells within her. Blessed is the soul who goes down into that abyss and so enters into possession of the treasures she possesses there.

The spiritual life is also the dwelling of ourselves in God, escape from self, rapture. It is indeed, in another sense, that fundamental conversion which causes the soul, centred upon itself, to turn from self towards the Word. It is that escape from self by which the soul breaks through the limits of its nature in order to enter into the sphere of the Trinity, relying upon the powerful grace of the Word, like Abraham leaving his country and family—that is to say, the universe of familiar things—to set out for the Promised Land and travel towards an unknown world, a world which ever remains an unknown world. For God remains a mystery even while He shares Himself.

The spiritual life, then, is a personal relationship between the soul and the Word. In thus setting grace to work, in begetting Himself in the soul by a perpetual birth which is the spiritual life, the Word is revealed to the soul through its activity. Grace is the sweet odour that betrays the presence of the Word. It reveals to the soul the presence of the Word, and encourages the soul to seek for the Word. And so we find here once again, but at a higher level, that action of the Word which through more and more exalted works manifests Himself to the soul, awakens it from slumber and urges it forward through the night in a quest that grows ever more ardent, striving to seize upon Him who ever eludes the grasp, and whom it demands in vain from the guardians of the city.

These upliftings which God prepares in human hearts are the spiritual pilgrimage itself. He takes the baptized soul in whatever state it is, still involved in the habits of the flesh, in that deep pit of misery inherited from sin. He releases it from its guilty bonds by arousing in it displeasure at sin and pleasure in the law of God. 'If you have any love for me, you must keep the commandments which I give you.'[1] The property of the action of the Word will be at first to give rise to such conformity with the will of God, to draw the soul towards the following of the Commandments, to give it a horror of sin. This is the first sign of the action of the Word in the soul. He will reproach the soul when it is pursuing evil ways, and encourage it when it turns towards good. And the spirit of evil works in the opposite way. This is what spiritual experience teaches us, from the *Shepherd of Hermas* to the *Exercises* of Ignatius Loyola.

Thus the Word of God, which manifests Himself to the soul according to its needs, and tempers Himself to its capabilities, first becomes a physician to those who are sick. The soul displays its wounds so that He may heal them. He opens the eyes of the blind, He gives hearing to the deaf. A life that is still sluggish awakens little by little from sleep. Whilst the carnal soul is only delighting in carnal things, the Word gives the Holy Spirit which stirs up the spiritual life and invites the soul to take pleasure in

[1] St. John 14 [15].

spiritual things. All the bruises of sin, all the twisting and arrogance, all the indifference and hardness, give way little by little beneath the touch of grace to the awakening of new life, the unfolding of the spiritual man.

. . . . .

Then the Word leads the healed and unified soul into the wilderness to teach it. 'It is but love's stratagem, thus to lead her out into the wilderness; once there, it shall be all words of comfort.'[1] The wilderness is that loss of earthly food which accustoms the soul little by little to feed upon every word that proceeds out of the mouth of God. Human realities which had played an exclusive part are now shown to be not illusory, but of secondary importance. On the other hand, spiritual blessings are perceived in all their fullness. In the quickening light of Christ, the soul is greatly enlarged. She exercises her spiritual faculties, she enters into the enjoyment of the theological virtues which are the source of spiritual activity. And this is always a divine work. 'The love of God has been poured out in our hearts by the Holy Spirit, whom we have received.'[2] The Word, like the pillar of fire and the rock of living water which accompanied the Jews in the wilderness of the Exodus, accompanies the soul in the wilderness of the abandonment of self, in that unknown world which flees from the entanglements of the natural life. For the wilderness is precisely this—a cessation from natural activity, and a condition of spiritual activity which causes the soul to follow the Word.

This journeying through the wilderness is to be in the state of passing from the level of the flesh to the level of the spirit. When Christ tells His Apostles that He is about to leave them, sorrow fills their hearts. They imagine that

[1] Osee 2 14.   [2] Rom. 5 5.

all will be lost if Jesus is hidden from the grasp of their senses, if they lose His visible presence. But Jesus explains to them that to pass, as He is about to do, from the level of the earthly to the level of the heavenly, is to pass to a greater reality, and that this is the very work He came to perform. Now what takes place in Christ takes place also in the soul. When Jesus hides Himself from sense-experience, the soul too imagines that she is forsaken. But Jesus explains that this is the necessary condition for passing from the level of the flesh to the level of the spirit. 'Why are you seeking one who is alive, here among the dead?'[1]

Thus the movement of the spiritual life follows the very movement of the economy of the mystery of Christ. The Word of God has come looking for the dead soul, as He came looking for dead humanity at the Incarnation. He was the Inward Master who taught the soul His ways and truths, as He personally taught the Apostles during His ministry. Now he conceals Himself from the soul in the night of spiritual trial, as He withdrew from the presence of His Disciples in the Passion. And just as the Apostles, even after the warnings of their Lord, were bewildered by His disappearance, so too the soul, in her hunger for knowledge, in her still fleshly nature, is tempted to despair at that apparent absence. The period of trial is itself a proof of the love of the Word for the soul, since it is necessary to deprive her of visible things and encourage her to turn towards those good things which are invisible.

The soul must live, then, by pure faith. She no longer possesses visible benefits, nor does she yet enjoy those that are invisible. The word of God is her sole support. And it is precisely on this trust that she must learn to rely. She must never rely in the least upon herself, but solely

[1] St. Luke 24 [5].

upon the Word. Every day He gives her the food she needs, but she should rely on Him for the future. If she tries to lay up stores of manna, it will go rotten. Thus the soul becomes accustomed to being at the mercy of the Word. Experience gradually convinces her that He deserves her trust. She no longer tries to hold on to the past. She understands that what she is given now is always better than what was given before, So she moves forward, leaning upon her Bridegroom. She 'makes her way up by the desert road, leaning upon the arm of her true love.'[1] The desert is the place of the spiritual ascension; but that ascension is only achieved by 'leaning upon the arm of her true love.' And it makes an exclusive claim upon the soul to rest entirely upon Him in a region where she can do nothing by herself.

Thus, in proportion as the soul moves forward through the desert, the action of the Word increases and that of the soul declines. On the level of the correction of its failings and the acquisition of virtues, the will, stirred up by grace, plays an active part. But here it does little but consent. For it is the Word who does everything. This is the sleep to which the Song of Songs refers: 'I lie asleep; but oh, my heart is wakeful.'[2] Formerly the Word had but to awaken the soul from spiritual sleep. But now it is in the slumber of the senses, the cessation of all fleshly activity, in a complete respite, in the silence of the night, that the Birth of the Word is brought to pass. The heart alone is wakeful— that is to say, the centre of the soul is summoned to an absolutely simple act of waiting upon the Word, to a consciousness of presence beyond every other consciousness, to a simple loyalty to the wondrous action which is taking place in her.

[1] Song of Songs 8 5.   [2] Song of Songs 5 2.

This desert of the mind is also the desert of the will. The soul unlearns self-will and self-determination. She no longer knows what she desires. Or rather she desires only what her Beloved desires. She enters into sublime detachment, which is no longer to will anything except what God wills. She entrusts herself wholly to God in everything that concerns her. Thus she enters into a very deep and intimate state of dying to herself, which enables her to see the mysterious designs of God. She wills what God wills. Her charity is enlarged till it embraces all things. And that charity is actuated by a wholly spiritual energy, free from the limitations of the flesh, and sharing in the work of the Divine Charity.

In this way the mystery of Christ takes place in the individual soul. The Passion leads to the Resurrection and the Ascension. These mighty acts of God, prefigured in the Old Testament, substantially fulfilled in Christ, radically communicated by baptism, attain their effect in the soul, before having their final repercussion in the body itself at the Resurrection. There is nothing forced in this analogy. It only expresses the action of the same Trinity at different moments in the history of salvation. But these actions themselves have a mutual relation. They are only parts of the same design that is fulfilled according to the purposes of Divine Wisdom, according to the power of irrevocable Righteousness, according to the design of merciful Love.

.   .   .   .   .

The soul which He came to find, which He taught and trained, which He purified in the blood of His Passion, which He caused to appear before Him holy and immaculate, is finally conducted by the Word into His Father's House to celebrate an eternal union. This supreme work was already substantially included in baptism, which was already a covenant. But while the gift that Christ made of Himself to the soul was already boundless, the gift which the soul made of herself to Christ was still weak and uncertain. It was necessary for the soul to be tried in the testing fire, so that her love might be strengthened by opposition, and the life of the spirit should reach maturity in her person. In this way, the Word brought to its fulfilment in the soul the gift which He had made to her in the baptismal character, but into the full possession of which she must enter stage by stage.

This emphasizes first of all on the level of personal experience the part played in God's plan by time. We have already established this on the level of the history of salvation as a provision of the Divine Wisdom which orders all things. But it is on the level of the individual soul that we can understand its meaning from the standpoint of the conditions of the individual. We can see, in fact, that God proportions His gifts to the capacity of the receiver; for the work which He pursues is not one which takes place in the darkness apart from man, it is the giving of freedom, for the only thing that is of value in His eyes is love freely given. Thus does it become necessary for the soul, entreated by this first unsought-for grace, to welcome and respond to this grace so as to become fit for a greater grace.

This forms part of the very basis of creation. It is that man whom He has created, that the Word comes to save. Now if His working in man were such as to demand nothing from man, the latter would be a bystander and merely the object of God's Transcendence. The *Soli Deo gloria*, while treating human freedom as so absurd that God pays no regard to it, strives towards the glory of God, which is, says St. Irenaeus, the living man. For all contempt for creation is contempt for God the Author of Creation.

Now freedom is the summit of creation. In the Christian scheme of things it is given full consideration. This can be seen in point of fact both in the price God sets upon it and in His refusal to violate it.

And here it is the story of man that illuminates the history of mankind, whilst from the point of view of the action of God it is the history of salvation that illuminates the life-story of the individual. For we can certainly see at work in the history of mankind a system of training similar to that which is at work in the life-story of the individual. Thus it is, as we have said, that Irenaeus shows us the Word being tempered to what man can bear, slowly accustoming him to the divine ways before revealing Himself more fully in the Incarnation. The action of the Word appears therefore as a prolonged training which first of all, by means of the Law, makes ready a will as yet undisciplined, so as to make it capable one day of a free commitment to a life of Grace.

This raises an essential point in relation to the action of the Word, one that is at the very heart of this chapter—His action in human liberty. For after making ready the whole economy of salvation and setting it to work in its essential shape, it now becomes necessary to bring it to fulfilment by the conversion of men's free-wills. And this is still the work of the Word. Yet even though it is the work of the Word, it is still the work of freedom. It would be a strange paradox if, in proportion as a man is further actuated by the Word, he were to become so much the less free, that is, less himself. It would be strange indeed if grace were to destroy man's nature and set him cheek by jowl with an uncongenial creation. But this would be to misunderstand the Incarnation at its final stage, at the level of its operation in every soul. It would be to go back to the divided nature upon which grace was superimposed. At the level of the individual Christian, this would be to return to the distinction between the noumenal Jesus and the phenonenal Jesus.

This is what we often find to-day. For many thinkers, there is a temptation to set faith and occurrence, the natural man and the supernatural man side by side. They see a parallelism without reciprocal action between the two modes, which correspond without ever coming together. Pure supernaturalism is set beside pure naturalism. They are so anxious not to contaminate God with man that they want to see the acts of God only in God Himself, and not in man. And there is an equal anxiety not to contaminate man with God, to preserve the 'divine' character and to maintain with jealous zeal the natural, political, psychological, and philosophical orders each in its absolute autonomy.

Now this is to misunderstand the very nature of the Incarnation, which is the act by which the Word of God, hustling through the hierarchy of essences, comes down into the world of man to grasp human nature without being confounded with it, so as to set it to work in a divine manner by lifting it up above itself. It is just the same with the mind. The Word of God comes to make contact with the human mind working as it does within the limits of space and time; and by conveying to it a mode of divine operation, He acclimatizes it to divine things and makes it capable of knowing God with the knowledge with which God knows Himself, first of all in darkness, possessed by faith, and one day in the light of vision. This higher fulfilment of the mind is not a violence done to it, but the supreme achievement of the mind, the kingly understanding of the sons of God, the gift of Wisdom.

It is the same, too, with freedom. The freedom which the

Word comes seeking is not an abstract freedom. It is a freedom involved in the flesh, a captive freedom. It is this that the lifegiving Word seeks in its imprisoned state, and which He first liberates from its bonds. For freedom is not at the beginning, but at the end; it is not freedom of choice, indifferentiation, but the ability of the will to realize what is willed, to grasp its own fundamental finality, to realize its own spiritual nature. This is where Marxism is right in defining freedom as liberation. But it sets that liberation only against the background of economic slavery—and it remains to be seen whether at this level it is liberation at all. Real misery goes deeper. Only the Word destroys the spiritual slavery of deep-seated sin, the mysterious power of the Prince of this world.

This then is freedom, which the Word trains first through the Law, and then establishes and strengthens. It is the equivalent of the Old Testament in the story of the individual. Then, when it is strong enough, He frees it from enslavement to the Law and summons it to move towards its end with its own proper spontaneity. Even when it is trained in the virtues, He drives it on to a higher training by leading it from within to perform higher acts, and by bestowing upon it the means that will enable it to achieve them. By acting within the individual soul, the Word simply carries freedom to its highest fulfilment. His action does not destroy it, but fulfils it.

The perfecting of freedom by grace finds its supreme expression in that strengthening of freedom such as belongs to the soul consumed by the life of love, established by God in permanent giving and receiving, withdrawn henceforth from misfortunes, recollected and as if hidden in the sanctuary of the Trinity, established within God in Christ through the mystical union. Nothing can any longer have power over it. Who can separate it from the love of Jesus ? There is no longer even any impatience with the last veils that hide the Beloved. The soul henceforth accepts the delay that separates it from the vision in a wholly peaceful placing of self in the hands of the Beloved. He is the soul's, and the soul is His. And this certainty establishes it in that utter peace which alone will enable the sun of vision to shine.

Having come to this final state with Christ, hidden in Him in the Trinity, the soul finds in herself the perfection of the fullness of mystery. And as the glorious Manhood of Christ, raised up to God, bestows Fatherly blessings for distribution to mankind—*Dedit dona hominibus*—so the soul, wedded to the Word, receives as a dowry all the possessions of her Bridegroom, which she distributes in her turn, sharing divine gifts from that life, working out the salvation of the world invisibly with Christ, mysteriously associated with the purposes of divine Love. Her open hands are full of grace. Rays leap from her hands. But if she shares gifts that are not hers, it is indeed she who distributes them.

The consummation of the work of the Word in the soul thus serves to make it not only full of peace, but itself a source of grace. This is how, as Clement of Alexandria has said, the soul becomes truly the image and likeness of God, who gives love freely. The soul already begins to perform heavenly deeds, although its body remains on earth. The same Curé d'Ars whom calumnies overwhelmed, whose lack of ability tortured him, who dragged his 'carcase' about, is the man who bestows upon souls the illumination, counsel, and guidance which produce conversion and sanctification, and whose wonder-working power often reaches the limits of the cosmos, the frontiers of the Resurrection.

Now the paradox is that it is when the soul is wholly established in the good that at last it feels utterly free. The final chains are broken. Nothing any longer restricts the pure actuality of love. Now the pure actuality of love is for the soul her proper end. The soul henceforth moves freely in the world without any hindrance. Even that ontological weakness which characterizes creation as such, that gap between the person and the good, that mixture of being and nothingness, without which he would not be a creature, and which even made the possibility of evil a corollary of created existence—it is by these that the action of the Word fills up all the gaps, so to speak, strengthening her in the good till she is already inchoately initiated into an enjoyment of goodness which glory shall ratify for ever.

The elimination of the possibility of sin is the supreme work of the Word which will be fulfilled in glory. It raises creation to a mode of divine existence, by enabling it to share in the very changelessness of God. This is what Origen failed to see, when he thought that the possibility of sin, since it formed part of the essence of creation, must therefore always remain, and that further Falls were always possible. But this was to misunderstand the perfection that grace adds to creation. The freedom which is in grace is not a lesser freedom, but a freedom delivered from the congenital weakness of a created freedom, which is qualified not as something liberated, but as something created. God, by raising created freedom above its created condition, causes it to share in the changelessness of un-created freedom.

.   .   .   .   .

Thus the spiritual life enables us to rediscover the work of the Word beneath its various aspects and in its ultimate action. It is a work of the Trinity, dwelling in the soul and dwelt in by the soul. It is a sharing in the divinized humanity assumed by the Word, whose body and pleroma it is. It takes place in the setting of the Church and the Sacraments, which provide its immediate condition. It also represents the end of the work of the Word, the completion of the act by which He came to seek for human freedom in order to lead it towards His Father and thus raise up the True Temple, built of living stones, the True Paradise planted with those trees of life that are the saints.

BIBLIOGRAPHY

F. BERTRAND, *Mystique de Jésus chez Origène*, Paris, 1951.

J. DANIÉLOU, *Platonisme et théologie mystique*, Paris, 1954.

ST. AUGUSTINE, *Confessions*. (Many versions.)

ST. BERNARD, *Sermons on the Song of Songs*.

TAULER, *Sermons*.

ST. JOHN OF THE CROSS, *The Spiritual Canticle*. (Complete Works, London, 1947.)

ST. IGNATIUS LOYOLA, *Journal Spirituel*, Paris, 1958.